The Spelling Book

Teaching Children How to Spell, Not What to Spell

Gladys Rosencrans
Delta School District 37
Delta, British Columbia, Canada

INTERNATIONAL Reading Association

800 Barksdale Road, PO Box 8139

Newark, Delaware 19714-8139, USA

www.reading.org

The International Reading Association attempts, through its publications, to provide a forum for a wide spectrum of opinions on reading. This policy permits divergent viewpoints without implying the endorsement of the Association.

Director of Publications   Joan M. Irwin
Managing Editor, Books and Electronic Publications   Christian A. Kempers
Associate Editor   Matthew W. Baker
Assistant Editor   Janet S. Parrack
Assistant Editor   Mara P. Gorman
Publications Coordinator   Beth Doughty
Association Editor   David K. Roberts
Production Department Manager   Iona Sauscermen
Graphic Design Coordinator   Boni Nash
Electronic Publishing Supervisor   Wendy A. Mazur
Electronic Publishing Specialist   Anette Schütz-Ruff
Electronic Publishing Specialist   Cheryl J. Strum
Electronic Publishing Assistant   Peggy Mason

Library of Congress Cataloging in Publication Data
   Rosencrans, Gladys.
   The spelling book: Teaching children how to spell, not what to spell / Gladys Rosencrans.
      p.   cm.
   Includes bibliographical references (p.) and index.
   1. English language—Orthography and spelling—Study and teaching (Elementary).   I. Title.
LB1574.R654   1998   98-23708
372.63'2—dc21
ISBN 0-87207-192-8 (pbk.)

Second Printing, October 1999

In loving memory of my mother Lil Altin,
a wonderful teacher whose joy in life was helping children.

C O N T E N T S

P R E F A C E

The *Spelling Book: Teaching Children How to Spell, Not What to Spell* is the result of a voyage of inquiry that grew out of personal frustration. I have spent many years working with children with learning disabilities and my empathy for them has grown with each student and passing year. Spelling is the bane of many students' lives. Writing is the indicator of success in our school system and these students, from their earliest experiences, have not succeeded. Their worth has typically been equated with their ability to demonstrate their knowledge through correct spelling. The remedial programs we have devised have too often had little effect on real success. The pragmatic writing of students in these programs continues to be riddled with errors, and spelling tests continue to be a source of frustration and embarrassment.

Although children with learning disabilities are the most conspicuous example of this problem, the trend is evident in regular classrooms too. The names of the students on the top of the spelling chart and those who ace the spelling tests or are selected for spelling bees usually do not change over the years. Good spellers continue to be good spellers and poor spellers continue to struggle.

Many teachers share the frustration of these struggling students and have tried, to the best of their knowledge, to lessen the pain. They have worked diligently with the students during proofreading conferences, fixing all the mistakes and transforming the piece of writing into a sea of pencil marks. This coaching generally entails reviewing phonics rules, having the child sound out the word, looking up the word in the dictionary, or providing the correct spelling. When this fails to work, teachers engage a specialist or resource teacher (such as myself) to fix the problem. Specialists typically

- do more of the strategies just listed, but in an intensive small-group setting,

- deliver an exhaustive phonics program in which each rule is drilled to mastery (which is evident at least in the skill and drill exercises and tests),
- implement a sight-word program in which students memorize words and add them to their repertoire, and finally
- teach the child memory strategies to help him or her "learn" the words, at least for the spelling test.

Corrective instruction often is combined with suggested adaptations for the classroom teacher, most often reducing the number of words for which the child is responsible on the spelling test. Reducing the number of words is an interesting response to the problem. It has been implemented out of sympathy for the child, to avoid damaging self-concept still further. But what is the implicit message for the child? "I'm dumb. I can't do as many words as everyone else." This message is unavoidable and is reinforced continually because in spite of our efforts, writing and tests continue to be filled with mistakes.

All of the strategies discussed in the preceding paragraph have been used with the very best of intentions and sometimes the students have actually enjoyed the activities used to teach them. They have been commonly presented in game format and each student has received compassionate individual attention along with the spelling practice. Unfortunately, however, our efforts have not had the desired effect—many children still cannot spell.

A desperate wish to break this cycle of failure for students like Amy, a wonderful, talented young girl who worked so hard to *get it right*, led me to write this book. Having gradually developed professionally from teaching language as a series of sequential skills to an appreciation of whole language theory, I knew that trying to teach spelling as isolated exercises was not going to work. I believed that children would learn spelling best as they engaged in real writing activities, but knew from my experience with children like Amy that they were unlikely do so without direct instruction. But what kind of instruction was going to be effective?

Parents were a catalyst in my developmental process. I remember my many interviews with Amy's mother, Anne. She would challenge my thinking with questions like "But *how* is she going to learn to spell if we don't drill the rules and practice for the test?" Obviously, and with good reason, simply telling her to encourage Amy to write often was not going to satisfy her. My quandary led me to join a teacher action-research group with the goal of finding effective ways to teach spelling to struggling learners. One thing led to another, and a master's thesis in spelling and this book were the result.

To begin my research, I began to read everything I could get my hands on about both traditional and whole language theories of spelling instruction. I quickly came to realize that both ideologies were based on valid research and that they were not necessarily as contradictory as they initially appeared. Children do need to learn about the alphabetic, or phonetic, basis of the English language and the rules or generalizations that govern it, but these skills need to be learned within the context of real writing for application to occur. It is not enough for children to learn *about* spelling, they need to learn to *write* effectively. The program goal had to move away from memorizing words to pass a test to learning how to spell unknown words during the writing process. The *how-to* seemed to be the piece that was missing from spelling instruction. We teach children about the writing process, the reading process, and math processes, so why don't we use direct instruction to teach them about the processes that good spellers use? If we want children, especially those who struggle, to be strategic, metacognitive spellers, we need to focus our teaching on these strategies. Some theoretical work had been done in this area by researchers such as Mary Tarasoff and Bernice Wong, but the question remained of how to incorporate practical, classroom-applicable methods.

Although my work was originally focused on children with learning disabilities, I believed that the most effective place for real learning was in their regular classroom where they were engaging in real writing, not down the hall in the resource room. I also came to realize that the kind of strategic teaching I was promoting was good instruction for all, not just challenged spellers. So I enlisted the support of Amy's regular classroom teacher, Catherine Ross, and she invited me to try out my ideas in her Grade 4–5 classroom. We tried different lessons, rejected ideas that didn't work, reviewed progress, and found that we were having very promising results. Test scores were improving, but more important, there was significant evidence of application in independent writing for all students. Using Catherine's class as a springboard, I have used the methodologies included in this book with many other classes and with students in resource rooms and have had continued success. As the strategies were used and documented, *The Spelling Book* began to take shape as more of an instructional methodology than a lockstep sequential program. It continues to grow and develop with each new classroom or group because the instruction is an integral part of the writing program and is planned in response to the needs specific to the group.

The Spelling Book is dedicated to all those students like Amy who had to work so hard at spelling, to parents like Anne who cared so much and challenged me to put my money where my mouth was about how to teach their children, and to teachers like Catherine who welcomed me into their classrooms and helped me to field-test my ideas because they too want to ease the pain of laboring to spell. I hope you will be able to take the ideas suggested here, shape them to your particular group of children, and teach them how to spell, not what to spell.

Teaching Spelling: An Introduction

Spelling may not be the most critical part of the elementary school curriculum nor even the primary focus of the writing program, but it surely can (and does) cause a lot of frustration for poor spellers, for their parents, and for their teachers. It also provides fodder for media commentary on educational practice.

One problem with spelling is that it is so visible. A quick glance at a story, report, or any piece of writing quickly reveals errors, at least to a competent speller. The content need not even be read for the errors to be seen. In addition, writing quality is difficult to evaluate objectively. There is little that is definitely good or bad. Spelling is, therefore, an easy target for emphasis in evaluation, because one seems to be able to say with relative confidence that spelling is correct or incorrect. Parents are prone to focus on this visible attribute. Allowing children to write without correcting spelling errors, even in journals, has been the subject of much concern. Children (and teachers) are often chastised for the spelling errors (Diakiw, 1991). Because parents often do not have the luxury of training in language development and are unaware of the higher-level thinking and writing skills the teacher is trying to achieve, their evaluation of the writing process is restricted to spelling.

There is no question that the ability to spell correctly is not a valid measure of intelligence, nor even of topic knowledge. It is not easy, however, to ignore spelling errors. Try to appreciate the feelings of the child who has labored to express important thoughts, only to have the work rejected for the quality of the spelling; or the child whose weak short-term memory consistently results in failing grades on the weekly spelling test; or even the child who has a good memory and aces the spelling test, but whose independent writing is riddled with errors. Inhibiting? You bet! And parents and teachers who allow their frustration with challenged spellers to surface too often make matters worse, compounding an already poor self-concept.

To Teach or Not to Teach Spelling?

Research into the area of written language development presents opposing viewpoints. Whole language theorists are often cited as suggesting that no formal spelling be taught (Groff, 1986). They argue that through immersion in a language program rich in independent writing children will learn to spell through a natural progression. Traditionalists argue that direct instruction, phonics rules, and a structured, sequential word-study program are necessary. Classroom practice usually reflects the teacher's current philosophy based on personal research, perceived student need, and public opinion. Such diverse viewpoints, both based on viable research, often have confused teachers. Practice therefore, is polarized, with some teachers adopting an informal, holistic approach and others opting to teach traditional spelling programs as a segment of their language arts program.

Informal Instruction

One common reaction in schools is not to teach spelling in a traditional, formal way. This practice does not necessarily suggest that spelling is not being addressed, but rather that children are encouraged to learn to spell by writing instead of through traditional, isolated spelling exercises (Bean & Bouffler, 1987). Research has suggested that spelling develops most effectively when children are provided with many opportunities to use spelling in a meaningful way. Gentry (1987) and others contend that experimenting with and using language to express real ideas will enable children to internalize the idiosyncrasies of the English language and support their progress through the stages of spelling development. This theory holds that trying to memorize all the rules of grammar and phonics, which are often inconsistent, is of questionable value. In fact, this memorization may even inhibit natural progression. Some theorists suggest that no formal instruction be planned, but that instruction be provided as the need occurs. Ideally, these teachable moments are seized during writing conferences. This type of instruction is known as *informal* or *incidental*, and there is no question that many children will become proficient writers using it. Many children, however, will not.

In classrooms there is often insufficient time to provide the necessary help for struggling spellers. A personal writing conference may occur once a week or less often and usually is not more than 5 to 10 minutes long. It is debatable whether this amount of time will sufficiently cover all of the inconsistencies and gaps in spelling knowledge that may be present. Too often the result is dependent students who wait for the teacher or another expert to proofread their work for them before moving to good copy, and who never learn to become independent spellers.

Formal Instruction

The other approach to teaching spelling that is practiced currently is an increased emphasis on formal spelling instruction. Many teachers have reverted to, or have never progressed beyond, the traditional spelling textbook, often for lack of anything to replace it. Unfortunately, much of the time spent in traditional spelling programs has been found to be of questionable value, and many of the strategies used may inhibit natural development (Hillerich, 1982). The largest percentage of time is often spent on issues not related to teaching spelling, such as classroom management and marking books and in correcting worksheets or workbooks. The most common weekly spelling format consists of a pretest, followed by a set of word-study exercises, and finally a posttest, which usually takes place on Friday. This sequence focuses on a predetermined list of words, which have been well established by research. High-frequency words found consistently in children's writing have been identified, as well as lists of common errors at all grade levels (Thomas, 1979). These words have been grouped into weekly lists to provide study in a sequenced set of skills. Excellent lists of phonetic word families have been developed (McCracken & McCracken, 1985) and words are often selected from thematic units.

Unfortunately, such traditional spelling programs have had less than optimum effectiveness (Graves, 1976). They have changed little over the decades, continue to focus on isolated phonetic and structural rules, and promote the attitude that the sole purpose of learning to spell is to pass the test on Friday. Good spellers tend to get better, and challenged spellers continue to struggle—not only on the tests but in their writing as well.

An Alternative Method of Spelling Instruction

Both formal and informal methods of teaching spelling have a good basis in research and have been designed to improve spelling ability in children. Yet there are difficulties with both approaches. Traditional methods do not take into account understandings of how children learn and apply their growing knowledge. Although children do learn many skills and rules using this method, much of the instructional time is spent in "busy work" or in memorization for tests, rather than in the application of spelling knowledge in real, independent writing. On the other hand, whole language theory does not seem to have been developed to the point of effective, implementable teaching strategies that can realistically be incorporated into the classroom. Not all children develop naturalistically without some prompts and guidance.

To ensure that children receive the support they need, our job as teachers is to identify key ingredients of successful instruction and incorporate these into a classroom spelling program that enables all children to develop their ability to spell. Although specific and direct spelling instruction can be productive, there has got to be a better method than these two polarized forms of spelling instruction. The ideas presented in this book attempt to describe a more successful way to help children become real spellers: ways to teach spelling, not memorization; ways to help children to learn *how* to spell, not *what* to spell; ways to structure activities to help children create their own understanding of our language. These ideas can actually be implemented in a real classroom with limited time and resources.

To accomplish this task of helping children become fluent writers, we need to teach and provide practice in successful application of the spelling strategies used by efficient spellers. A brief overview of current research that explains the basis on which the program was designed has been included in Chapter 2. From this research come the assumptions about learning that shape the lessons and program elements. A more detailed description of the strategies and attitudes necessary for effective spelling are given in Chapter 4.

The goal of *The Spelling Book* is to help students develop the confidence and ability to express their thoughts fluently using written language. This is done by providing direct instruction in the strategies that good spellers use as well as to develop word knowledge appropriate to their developmental level.

Assumptions About Learning

The ideas and strategies included in this book grew out of a basic list of assumptions about how children learn to spell. It is important to understand these assumptions because they provide the foundational philosophy and therefore drive the goals of the lessons that are the sometimes subtle difference from traditional spelling programs. These goals include developing metacognition, learning about the process of spelling rather than supplying the right answer, and developing understanding instead of remembering rules. I have included the list of assumptions that follow so that the reader can use them as a filter through which to monitor their instruction. They should provide the answer to the reflective question "Why am I doing what I am doing?"

Instruction should be frequent, planned, and purposeful. It is not good enough to leave learning to chance.

Ongoing assessment is an integral part of the learning process and provides impetus for instructional decisions. Because there is no lock-step sequence in learning to spell, lesson planning must be based on observed need.

Instruction should be geared to the developmental level of the learner. All people learn in different ways and at different rates. Effective instruction attempts to match teaching techniques to learning levels and learning styles or intelligences.

Spelling is interrelated and interconnected with all strands of language arts and should not be taught in isolation. No aspect of language use operates or is learned apart from the whole. To ensure optimum learning rather than memorization, language must retain links to meaningful context. Learning about language is no substitute for using language.

Instruction should be focused on teaching a variety of effective spelling strategies rather than on memorizing words. All the words needed for writing cannot be memorized, and children need effective strategies for attempting new or unknown words as they are encountered. There is no one right method that works for all words in all situations, and the ultimate goal is to become a fluent writer, not to pass a test.

Correct spelling is the product of active engagement in a systematic process for ordering letters into meaningful words. This process entails active exploration of words and language; development of a positive, purposeful attitude; and establishment of effective strategies and monitoring systems.

Optimal learning is a social process that best occurs when children engage in both collaborative and independent work. Children learn effectively as they discuss with their peers, share thinking, problem solve, and participate in authentic literacy experiences.

A safe, nonjudgmental classroom climate that promotes risk taking is important for learning. Students must feel free to test their hypotheses about spelling in an atmosphere of support and an honest valuing of diverse thinking.

Program Elements

The program described in this book, although originally developed to specifically help the poor speller reach greater success, has been designed in and for the regular classroom. The ideas have been used within a variety of intermediate classrooms, all of which have included wide diversity. I can say with confidence that the strategies are workable. The data gathered as the program developed were very encouraging (Rosencrans, 1993). Students improved significantly in their ability to perform, not only on standardized spelling tests, but in their pragmatic writing. Most of the lessons also have been used in a remedial setting with small groups or individuals with equal success.

I have outlined the elements of the program here, including lesson formats, tools used in the program, and spelling strategies. More information on the proram elements will be found in Chapter 3.

Scheduled, Daily Instruction

- Short blocks of time each day are allocated to spelling instruction.
- The lessons are integrated within the language arts program and other curricular areas.
- Words for study come from books or themes currently in use in the classroom.
- Although word lists may be used for exploration, no predetermined list is designated to be "learned" at any time.
- Structured times may be scheduled blocks of 15–25 minutes; exploration activities integrated with other curricular lessons; or short, 5-minute lessons.

Further information about useful lesson techniques and formats is presented in Chapter 6.

Responsive Planning

Lesson content is selected on the basis of student need as identified through observation and ongoing assessment. Assessment is varied, broad based, and analytical in nature. It is geared to inform planning decisions rather than to obtain a score.

Spelling and Word-Study Lessons

Experiences are structured purposefully to provide opportunities for students to explore language and to make their own generalizations about its form, use, and structure. Lessons make extensive use of cooperative learning to provide maximum opportunities for students to engage in discourse about spelling strategies, to share their thinking, and to develop metacognitive awareness. Detailed information about specific guided word-study lessons is presented in Chapter 7.

There are a variety of lesson formats, and children are grouped according to the goals of the spelling lesson. Whole-group lessons introduce concepts, guide thinking, and share strategies. Small groups are used for exploration activities, problem solving, and guided discussion. Small-group and individual minilessons help meet specific needs identified from observation or writing analysis; these usually occur during writing conferences. Individual application is used for reflection on learning in Spelling Logs, for independent practice or skills and strategies, and for personal writing.

Spelling Tools to Use Across the Curriculum

Various tools are used both within and outside spelling lessons. I have included brief descriptions of them here; all are described in more detail in Chapter 3.

Spelling Logs. To develop metacognition, students engage in frequent paraphrasing and reflection of learning in notebooks called Spelling Logs; these notebooks are also used for guided word study

Word Banks. These personal dictionaries are used as a reference for writing and to record words that the student is currently using and wants to remember. Word Banks are student generated. They may contain story words, theme words, or occasionally teacher-suggested words. Spelling in Word Banks must be accurate, because they also contain the words used for spelling tests.

Spelling "Tests." "Tests" in *The Spelling Book* differ from typical tests in that they are really just structured times to practice applying spelling strategies. Although they provide information about student learning, they are not used for marks. Students cannot study for them, because they are written with a partner who chose the words for dictation at random from the student's Word Bank. Students mark their own tests and keep track of their progress.

High-Frequency Words

Students learn that some words occur often in writing, or have irregular spellings and are therefore worth spending time learning. Words designated high frequency may come from published lists or be student generated.

Generic Spelling Strategies

These strategies are procedures that may be used with any new words in any context. They give the writer steps to follow in attempting to spell an unknown word. Six specific spelling strategies are presented in *The Spelling Book*.

Students are given direct instruction in the use of each strategy, because no one strategy will be effective in all situations. They should be introduced to the spelling strategies early in the program and use the strategies to continue their language exploration and acquisition of word knowledge and skills. Detailed explanation of the six strategies and instructional suggestions are given in Chapter 4.

Ongoing, Analytic Assessment

Children's errors are never random, and they provide information about misconceptions that should inform instruction. Assessment should be broad based and varied, but must occur in authentic contexts. Further information on assessment practices is found in Chapter 5.

Setting the Stage for Spelling

Creating the environment for learning and establishing shared goals is essential to success. Information about introductory activities is described in Chapter 6.

Parents as Partners

Parents want to help their children develop their spelling competence but often do not have the expertise. They welcome concrete suggestions from the teacher. Information to share with parents is presented in Chapter 8.

Conclusion

The Spelling Book presents a method of spelling instruction that forms an integral part of the classroom curriculum. Instruction is not confined to a single text or discrete series of exercises but contains multifaceted elements woven through all language and content areas. These include a variety of lesson formats, spelling tools, and generic and specific spelling strategies. These elements reflect a philosophical basis that focuses not only on increasing word knowledge but on strategic application and attitude as well. The book is set up to provide a theoretical foundation and then specific strategies and lessons to put the theory into practice. The theory found in the next chapter is necessary to set the stage for the subsequent chapters that give direction to implementation.

2

What We've Learned From Research

R esearch in the past two decades has provided insights into how to help children learn more effectively. Studies based on numerous interviews and examples of children's writing have helped us to understand the strategies and processes that evolve during the development of spelling competence, suggesting how to improve our teaching practices. The findings at times may seem to conflict and have caused great debate among theorists (Groff, 1986), but it is important to make an attempt to incorporate the findings, however disparate, into classroom practice. With thought and effort, research findings may not be as contradictory as they initially appear.

This chapter is a synthesis of some of the research about how children learn to spell. The findings form the basis upon which this program has been designed.

Environment Matters

The classroom environment is the vehicle for student success. It is essential that it be a safe, welcoming place where children feel able to take risks and explore their own thoughts. Clear links have been established among motivation, self-concept, and learning success. Situations that are perceived as evaluative, as competitive, or as emphasizing distinctness promote apprehension and hinder task involvement. For example, in my classroom, following an activity in which students had shared their individual spelling strategies, a very challenged speller wrote *I learned that I can spell a lot more word that I that. I learned the mistakes they made some were the same as my.* These feelings of relief, and of knowing that mistakes are part of learning go a long way in promoting success.

These findings are no surprise, but they should prompt us to examine some of our classroom practices. Structured, formal exercises that have one right answer, are done in isolation, and are marked for the right answer are often sources of apprehension. Can we find better ways for children to grow and develop?

Cooperative Learning Works

One of the most effective ways to build a positive environment is through the use of cooperative learning activities. Group work creates an environment where expertise, understandings, and inquiry are shared, risks are taken, and attitudes are positive. It has been found to be effective in achieving both group and individual goals. No evidence has been found to suggest that high achievers are held back in group situations. Use of peer resources creates support networks that go beyond simply having a more able student tutor one who is struggling. Not only does the sense of camaraderie and belonging that is fostered enhance learning, but all students benefit because the opportunity to put concepts into words solidifies learning for the more able student and helps the less able student. Time on task is increased, as is the amount of one-to-one discussion among students. Students effectively model the mental maneuvers or internal process of their thinking for each other. This modeling will develop the flexibility and acceptance of risk taking that are crucial for growth.

Observation Leads to Learning

"Spelling conventions are truly understood and learned when [children] discover the conventions themselves" (Buchanan, 1989, p. 72). It would therefore seem sensible to develop activities that ensure children observe spelling structures. Guided discussions encourage personal generalizations that facilitate not only understanding, but also motivation to learn and apply this growing knowledge in new contexts. Learning occurs most effectively when students take ownership for their progress and are encouraged to apply and extend it. Ownership occurs when the material has personal relevance, as opposed to remembering it "because the teacher says so" or "to pass the test." Effective instruction provides scaffolds for learning and problem-solving strategies, rather than the answers. The motivation and personal involvement generated by having children reflect on and verbalize their knowledge *in their own words*, rather than by parroting rules will promote retention and application. The more real the tasks we set, the more real problem solving students will do, and the more relevant the educational process will be.

> Children learn best in an environment conducive to a positive self-esteem and active learning. Nonsegregated, open-ended lessons that encourage children to explore language at their own developmental stage and to make their own generalizations are optimum.
>
> *(Duffy, Roehler, & Herrmann, 1988; Scott, Hiebert, & Anderson, 1992)*

> Research has shown significantly greater achievement for all students using cooperative learning techniques, including students with special needs.
>
> *(Slavin, 1991; Villa & Thousand, 1988)*

It is important to remember, however, that for many students it is not enough to leave the development of these skills and attitudes to chance. Immersion in language will not, in itself, ensure that all children move through the spelling stages and become proficient spellers. Some get stuck and may need a little nudge. It is our job as teachers to provide the nudge by not only creating a learning-conducive environment, but by making sure dialogue takes place. This refers to both the internal, reflective dialogue (I think it should be...; Oh yeah. I have to double the *t*; I had better...) as well as the interactive dialogue (How do you spell...?).

> *Children learn and remember those things they discover for themselves and thus have a personal understanding of, more than those things they are told and expected to remember.*
>
> *(Borkowski, et al., 1992; Buchanan, 1989; Freppon & Dahl, 1991)*

Spelling Should Not Stand Alone

All too often children do not get the message we think we are giving because they absorb our attitude rather than our words. So it is with spelling lists and lessons. When spelling is taught isolated from real writing, and the assessment of it is based solely on a weekly test, it is natural that children will think that "spelling is for exercises, not writing" (Graves, 1976, p. 90). Interviews I have conducted with many classes and individuals reveal this to be alarmingly true. When asked what was important in spelling, responses such as "remembering the hard words" or "doing good on the test" were common.

Teach, Don't Proofread

The attitude of spelling as separate and of students not having control is reinforced when the teacher acts as proofreader and "blue pencils" children's work for them. Our conscious goal is to develop independent, confident, purposeful spellers. However, we may inadvertently by our actions and attitude be convincing students that they should study hard and memorize words for a test, while in real writing only the teacher or other expert has the power to get the words correct. *Independent* proofreading skills are among the most important to teach, model, and reinforce if we expect students to become self-sufficient, successful writers.

> *Spelling lists and lessons isolated from real writing give the message that the object of learning to spell is to "pass the test."*
>
> *(Graham & Miller, 1979; Graves, 1976; Stahl, 1992)*

Children Learn to Spell in Stages

Numerous research studies have shown spelling to follow a natural progression (see Figure 1 on the following page). Very young children use lines or random letters to write. The letters have little or no link to the sounds in the words. It should be noted that they are not spelling words, rather they are conveying a message. This may be referred to as the *prephonetic* stage. Children gradually learn to connect sounds to letters, first to individual letters, and then to more complex letter clusters. The *phonetic* and *graphophonic* stages reflect this growing connection between speech sounds and letter names. A few letter sounds are used in writing such as beginning or final consonants (for example, a child might write *DSR* for *dinosaur* or *CM* for *coming*). Gradually, more accurate sound-symbol relations begin to appear (*PLA* for *play* or *WOK* for *walk*). As the child moves past reliance on sound alone, more

FIGURE 1 Stages of Spelling Development

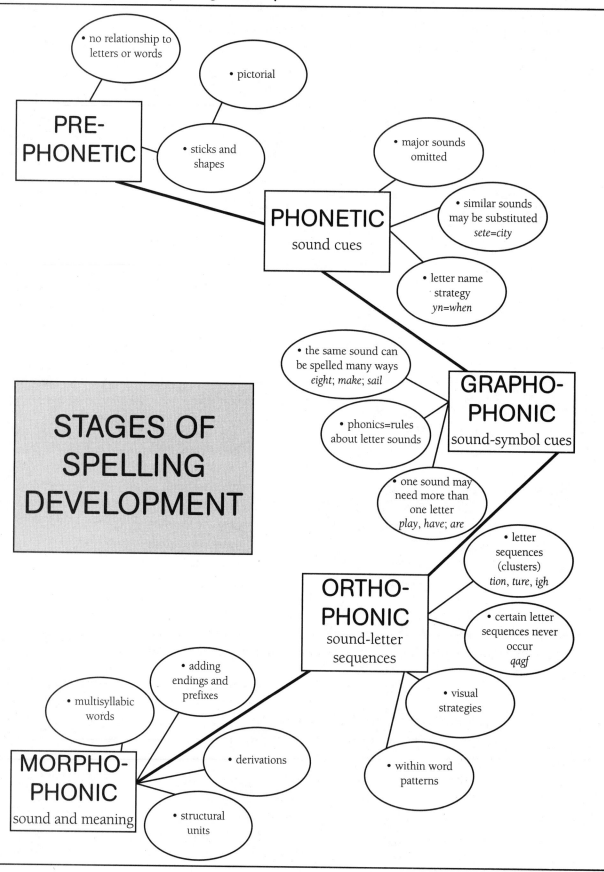

emphasis is placed on letter sequences or clusters that may not have a direct relation to letter sound (*ed* is pronounced "t"). The child also becomes more aware of the visual appearance of words. This may be described as the *orthophonic* stage. Overgeneralization of rules is common in this stage (for example, *HELPING* for *helping*) as awareness of orthographic structures continues to increase.

Word knowledge becomes more abstract in the *morphophonic* stage where semantic and syntactic information is used for applying higher-level phonics knowledge. Spellings begin to include multisyllabic words, derivations (such as *habit-habitual*), and the use of prefixes and suffixes all of which extend the *mental dictionary*, the knowledge that knowing one word means many words.

Activities that foster appropriate word knowledge can be structured to facilitate development in each stage (Buchanan, 1989). It would not be worthwhile to plan lessons in word derivatives for children at an early phonetic stage. Similarly, children who seem to be stuck in an overly phonetic stage when they should be past it need instruction in the use of other strategies to help them move on.

Spelling Is Not Magic

If children are going to be successful spellers, the process must be demystified for them. It is not magic, as many children think. There really is something that can be done to figure out how to at least attempt new words. As Palincsar and Ransom (1988) said, we need to change our classrooms from "mystery spots" to "thoughtful spots."

Expert spellers can identify a variety of strategies they use for spelling new words. These strategies range from visualizing the word, to saying it in parts, to sounding it out. These are strategies used while writing, not memorizing for a test. They may not ensure success, but they give a place to start. Creating an internal dialogue that says "I can try this…and if it doesn't work I will try…" may be challenging for some students, but the surprise and delight that occurs when children discover they really can spell "big words" (or at least get a lot closer than before) makes the effort worthwhile. Children do not need to memorize all of the 70,000 words in our language. There are strategies they can use with all words. Direct instruction in these generalizable spelling strategies, the goal of this program, will help children apply spelling to writing.

Spelling Means More Than Memorizing

Spelling is much more than just memorizing a predetermined set of words. It involves graphophonemic (letter-sound) relations, semantic (meaning-related) application, syntactic (grammatical) structure, and pragmatic (contextual) use of the word. It also involves the appearance of the word. To spell words, children must be able to isolate or discriminate individual sounds and be able to write the corresponding letters. Articulation and listening skills are an integral part of the spelling process, and then children

> *Spelling is developmental in nature. Children seem to progress systematically through increasingly sophisticated stages in their spelling knowledge.*
>
> *(Bean & Bouffler, 1987; Gentry, 1982; Templeton, 1979)*

> *Children need to learn how to spell, not what to spell. They need generalizable strategies that can be applied in all spelling contexts.*
>
> *(Beers, Beers, & Grant, 1977; Graves, 1976; Palincsar & Ransom, 1988)*

must be able to recognize when, or if, the correct spelling has been achieved. Variations such as homophones and dialect provide further challenges.

Spelling *is* a lot more than memorizing, and more than rules are needed to help students coordinate all this knowledge. Specific strategies are necessary to "activate spellers' schemata of words and to prompt them, to check accuracy" (Wong, 1986, p. 172). We too often assume that rules and knowledge will be applied in writing—but this is not necessarily the case. Children can be taught any number of rules or generalizations about our language, but to make sure the rules are actually applied students must be taught efficient, systematic techniques for spelling unknown words (Graham & Miller, 1979).

> *Spelling is a cognitive act that requires the coordination of several sources of knowledge.*
>
> *(Graham & Miller, 1979; Simon & Simon, 1973; Templeton, 1986; Wong, 1986)*

Teach Poor Spellers Effective Strategies

"What are the component processes that underlie skilled reading, math and writing?" (Wong, 1992, p. 152) is a question that has interested many researchers and prompted a number of studies investigating the strategic differences between good and poor spellers. Interviews, questionnaires, and writing analysis have revealed consistent observations. The strategies used by both good and poor spellers have been identified, and direct instruction can address many of them. We know that:

- Poor spellers report fewer strategies;
- Good spellers use visual imagery;
- Poor spellers sound words letter by letter;
- Good spellers break words into parts (not necessarily syllables);
- Good spellers think about smaller, known parts of words;
- Good spellers combine word segments with a visual image of the word;
- Good spellers use active monitoring or visual inspection;
- Good spellers actively pronounce words to cue auditory memory; and
- Good spellers tend to use phonics initially then add visual and semantic information.

It makes sense to teach all students to use the strategies of good spellers.

> *Strategic spellers sound out words in clusters, see little words in big words, visualize whole words, check for accuracy, and have metacognitive awareness and are able to verbalize their strategies.*
>
> *(Radebaugh, 1985; Rule, 1982; Wong, 1992)*

Students Need to Know the Why of Spelling

Metacognition is the awareness of effective personal learning strategies and the ability to monitor their success (Palincsar & Ransom, 1988). Put simply, it means the ability to figure out what to do when you have a problem (such as how to spell an unknown word), then to check to see if it worked. It also is the ability to try something else if the first strategy did not work. There is no one single successful strategy that will achieve correct spelling for all words and for all spellers. Accuracy demands the selection of the most appropriate strategy for a given word in a given situation and then at least one back-up strategy to try if the first one is unsuccessful. Therefore a variety of strategies, as well as an attitude that attaches importance to spelling, or a *spelling conscience*, is necessary for good spellers.

Explicit metacognitive instruction should be a part of each spelling lesson to ensure that students internalize the knowledge and apply it to personal writing in new contexts (Block & Peskowitz, 1990). This is especially true when we consider that poor spellers generally lack metacognition (Radebaugh, 1985). Spelling lessons will be better understood and more valued if students are encouraged to reflect on why they are learning a strategy and its other possible applications. The more students are able to understand their own learning process the more control they can take.

Teach Some Phonics

Phonics instruction is probably the most controversial topic in all language instruction and has caused the greatest debate (Groff, 1986), but even the most stringent whole language theorist would not dispute that a good knowledge of sound-symbol relations is beneficial in spelling. Phonics is the first strategy that is attempted in spelling a new word, and phonic knowledge seems to provide a "security base—something to build on" (Groff, 1979, p. 272). It would be unwise to adopt a take-it-or-leave-it approach (Lie, 1991; Stahl, 1992) to this obviously important skill. Our language is, after all, an alphabetic one. Research indicates that *phonemic awareness* (the ability to discriminate individual sounds in words) may be a major weakness for children who have difficulty in language learning (Stanovich, 1994). Training in sound discrimination has been found to improve spelling and reading success (Ball & Blackman, 1991; Lie, 1991).

The danger lies in teaching phonics rules as opposed to teaching spelling. There are 150–200 rules and being able to recite them does not equal spelling success. The usefulness of memorizing these phonics rules has often been questioned because of their incongruity. For example, Clymer (1963) found that 18 of 45 generalizations were consistently applicable. Many of the rules, particularly those pertaining to long vowels, have less than 50% reliability. Most errors cannot be corrected by phonics knowledge alone, but require visual and semantic information as well. Studies indicate that phonics instruction is meaningful only in conjunction with other, broader language experiences (Cramer, 1969; Paris & Jacobs, 1984). When error analysis reveals that most of a child's errors are phonetic in nature, it is probably not more phonetic information that is needed but other supplementary knowledge. Strategies that encourage the observation, awareness, and generalization of phonics rules within the context of natural reading and writing are a necessary component of effective spelling programs.

Visual Cues Support Phonics

English spelling really is an orderly and systematic schema, even though not always phonetically accurate. Phonics gives possible spellings, but they must be confirmed by semantic analysis (the meaning of the word) and by the visual appearance of the word (does it look right?). As children learn that spelling is based on more than the alphabet, they are better able to make sense of the language. They learn that some letter clusters have a variety of

> *Children need to be metacognitively aware of the variety of strategies that can be used to attempt to spell new words and to monitor accuracy.*
>
> *(Block & Peskowitz, 1990; Rule, 1982; Scott, Hiebert, & Anderson, 1992; Wong, 1986)*

> *A good knowledge of phonics facilitates successful spelling. The question is not whether to teach spelling, but how to teach it.*
>
> *(Ball & Blackman, 1991; Beers, Beers, & Grant, 1977; Cramer, 1969; Gentry, 1987; Lie, 1991; Simon & Simon, 1973; Stahl, 1992)*

sounds: *gh* as in *ghost*, enou*gh* and hi*gh*. Conversely, of course, many phonemes can be represented with different letters: for example *c*ause, d*o*ll, *s*alt. This is usually dependent on the surrounding letters, or where they are placed within the word. Predictability is brought to the words when one considers "within word patterns" and "meaning" (Templeton, 1986). Groups of letters have particular sounds depending on their position within words. For example, *gh* has a different sound when placed at the beginning of a word (*ghost*) than when placed at the end of a word (*enough*). Children can be guided to notice that *bl* is found at the beginning of words, but *ble* is found at the end, even though they have the same sound. Similarly, meaning has a significant impact in spelling. The best example is homophones that have the same sound but different spellings. The prepositional homophones *here*, *where*, and *there* all use the *ere* pattern. When students notice the semantic link it increases the preditability of language.

Spelling words with prefixes and suffixes makes sense only when the semantic relation is acknowledged. Research has revealed that seeing base words provides a more direct link with phonics than just hearing them. Words or word parts keep a visual relation to other words having similar meaning, even though the sound may change: for example, *medicine-medicinal* or *sign-signature*. Orthographic information or letter combinations seems to be more stable than phonetic information (Templeton, 1986), and children will see the similarities more easily than hearing them. Through this awareness comes a mental dictionary. These findings indicate benefits in structuring experiences that ensure children observe and discuss these orthographic patterns and their application in the spelling process.

Use Errors to Understand Children's Spelling Processes

Children rarely do anything without thought. Their attempts at spelling are based on their current perceptions of written language. Errors, if we take the time to analyze them, can help us to understand the child's thinking, and therefore plan better ways to nurture spelling development. For example, *yr, wtr*, and *wetar* are all attempts at the word *water.* Each reveals a different strategy use, however, and a different instructional need.

Analysis of writing samples is probably the most important evaluation tool for teachers because it examines how well skills and knowledge are being applied, the goal of a spelling program. *Miscue analysis* (Goodman, Watson, & Burke, 1987) has proven very effective in evaluating reading in real situations; the same process can be used to evaluate spelling.

Analysis of student writing, both edited and unedited (Buchanan, 1989) can provide a valuable source of information to determine both spelling knowledge and the processes by which children use this knowledge. It is useful because the quality of the student's spelling and the thinking that prompted it are examined. Information of this type provides more useful data upon which to make program decisions and future plans.

Structural and semantic (grammatical and meaning-related) patterns that reinforce the predictability of spelling should be a focus of spelling lessons as children move beyond the phonetic stages of development.

(Graves, 1976; Henderson & Templeton, 1986; Simon & Simon, 1973; Templeton, 1986)

A comprehensive assessment including a variety of measures should be conducted over time. Errors are a map to the thinking processes a child uses when spelling and from such analysis, many misconceptions can be identified and corrected. For example, proofreading ability, which is crucial to spelling competence, is only evident from examining errors. Student interviews are also useful in appraising strategic and metacognitive awareness, and dictated standardized tests cover a further dimension. A thorough child-centered approach to assessment may provide the missing link between current research and instructional practice. It generates lessons that focus on process as well as product and reflect analyzed need rather than lock-step, sequential exercises.

The errors children make as they write are neither random nor thoughtless. When examined diagnostically, they reveal systematic application of the child's level of understanding.
(Buchanan, 1989; Gentry, 1987; Tarasoff, 1990)

Conclusion

This chapter is a brief summary of the research related to spelling and learning. These findings generated the assumptions about learning upon which *The Spelling Book* was developed. As the chapter has explained, we need to keep the following key points in mind as we begin to plan for spelling instruction:

- Children need to learn the variety of strategies that good spellers use to write new words, in conjunction with learning about the phonological and orthographic structures of our language.

- Word knowledge and strategic application have equal importance in developing competence.

- Attitude is a crucial factor.

- Metacognition or awareness of appropriate strategies and the confidence to make attempts determine growth in spelling.

- The classroom environment plays a significant role in facilitating student success.

- A climate of trust, discovery, and cooperation is vital in ensuring that students are motivated and engage actively in exploring language.

The following chapters will describe how these key points can be put into practice.

Assessment should be comprehensive and eclectic. Spelling analysis from pragmatic writing, as well as from standardized word lists should be included. Information from student interviews is also of value.
(Buchanan, 1989; Scott, 1990)

If the goal of a spelling program is competence during writing, then evaluation should be based on analysis of independent writing samples.
(Buchanan, 1989; Gable, Hendrickson, & Meeks, 1988; Gentry, 1987; Radebaugh, 1985)

3

Spelling Goals: How and What Do I Want to Teach?

his book was designed for use with intermediate students. Instruction is provided as part of guided discussion and word study through both whole-class and cooperative group activities and individual writing conferences. The teaching methods described here include direct instruction in a variety of effective spelling strategies, how to develop awareness of indistinct factors influencing spelling success such as metacognition and integrated cueing systems, and examples of structured opportunities, which allow students to explore and conceptualize the complexities of the English language. To the greatest extent possible, this book advocates exploration that comes from current classroom activities, not from isolated exercises. The content of the lessons and any word lists used for word study will therefore come from words that are part of class themes or the language arts program. The lessons may be used repeatedly and with a variety of classes.

The spelling methodology described in *The Spelling Book* is not a lock-step series of sequential skills and exercises, but is an accumulation of structured activities and discussions. It is not intended to be followed in its entirety nor necessarily in the format presented, but is to be adapted and changed for every class in which it is used. Each group of children is unique in its stage of development, experiences, ability levels, and curriculum. Useful spelling instruction will reflect these differences. Using this methodology, instruction is planned and purposeful, with careful consideration of individual needs and situations.

Why Teach Spelling?

Why do you want to teach spelling? This question is not as facetious as it may sound. It is important to examine the reasons for trying to include spelling instruction in an already busy schedule. Just like children, we need to establish a purpose and to set the tone. It is also necessary to promote a positive mindset and a personal commitment. So, take a few minutes and reflect on the following questions:

- Why do you want to devote time to spelling?
- What is it that you want to accomplish?
- What do you want your students to be able to do?

I am willing to bet that your answers included things like:

- I want the students to spell when they are writing.
- I want them to have strategies to use when they are writing.
- I want them to understand how to spell and how our language is written.
- I want students to be able to express their ideas in writing without being hampered by spelling.
- I want to satisfy parents.
- I want students to develop a core vocabulary.

Next step: Think back to a time when you had to spell a difficult word. Try to articulate how you spelled it. What methods did you use? What went through your mind? Ask other people the same questions. You may be surprised at how many different replies you get. When I ask the questions at workshops, I can fill an entire sheet of chart paper with the suggestions that include: Sound it out, look at it, remember where I saw it, look it up in a dictionary, write it a bunch of different ways, write it in parts, say the syllables, think of the parts that I know, think of the phonics rules, and think of another word that is the same.

Thinking about these questions and their answers provides the goals of a good spelling program. We want to teach children strategies that they will be able to use to spell when they are writing for a purpose. Nowhere was passing the test or doing the exercises in the spelling book mentioned.

These same questions are important to ask parents as well, if we want their support. They want exactly the same things for their children that we do, but they may not have thought of it in terms of long-term goals. If we help them to do this, they are usually much more supportive.

Spelling Goals

The goal of this book is to better enable children to spell correctly when they are writing (see Figure 2). Remembering that the goal is not to have the child "pass the test," but rather to write conventionally, helps to shift the emphasis from memorization activities to spelling activities. It is not the list of words themselves that is important, but rather an understanding of how or why the words spelled. This book starts with the development of a personal motivation for learning to spell and an understanding of when spelling is important. Every lesson includes direct instruction in application to real writing.

Spelling lessons are designed to develop attitudes, skills, and knowledge that support children in learning how to spell correctly when it is important to do so, instead of how to memorize a few words for a test. Figure 3 outlines the specific objectives in these areas.

The Progression of Spelling Skills, Knowledge, and Attitudes

Figure 3 on the following page presents the specific skills, knowledge, and attitudes students should develop as they progress in spelling ability. Suggested times of introduction (1) and reinforcement (§) are given.

Figure 2 Spelling Program Goals

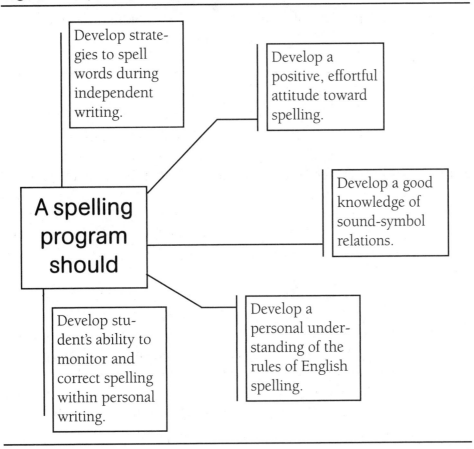

Figure 3 Expected Learning Outcomes in Spelling

Students will:	Early Primary Prephonetic	Phonic	Primary-Intermediate Graphophonic	Orthophonic	Intermediate Morphophonic
Attitudes					
recognize the contexts in which spelling is important.		1	§	§	§
develop a positive, effortful attitude.	1	§	§	§	§
develop a "spelling conscience."		1	§	§	§
develop an interest in words and spelling.	1	§	§	§	§
Skills					
learn to spell a variety of words frequently used in writing.		1	§	§	§
learn strategies applicable to spelling a variety of words.		1	§	§	§
apply spelling strategies in all writing activities.	1	§	§	§	§
monitor the accuracy of spelling while writing.		1	§	§	§
develop skills in proofreading.			1	§	§
develop strategies for learning and retaining the spelling of unusual or difficult words.		1	§	§	§
develop a mental dictionary, that is, extend knowledge of one word to spell another.			1	§	§
be able to verbalize effective spelling strategies and their application, also known as metacognition.		1	§	§	§
develop visual analysis skills.	1	1	§	§	§
predict spelling based on meaning.			1	§	§
Students will increase understanding of:					
Knowledge					
written words conveying meaning.	1	§	§	§	§
initial consonants.	1	§	§	§	§
final consonants.		1	§	§	§
medial consonants.		1	§	§	§
spacing between words.		1	§	§	§
consonant blends.		1	§	§	§
short vowel clusters such as *at*, *ash*, and *ent*.		1	§	§	§
regular double vowels such as *ee*, *ea*, and *ie*.			1	§	§
vowel clusters such as *ou*, *oi*, *ow*, and *au*.			1	§	§
soft *c* and *g*.			1	§	§
possessives.			1	§	§
complex clusters such as *ough*, *tion*, and *igh*.			1	§	§
multisyllable words.			1	§	§
punctuation.		1	§	§	§
capital letters.		1	§	§	§
plurals.		1	§	§	§
abbreviations.			1	§	§
contractions.		1	§	§	§
prefixes.			1	§	§
simple suffixes such as *ed*, *ing*, and *er*.		1	§	§	§
homonyms.			1	§	§
word origins.				1	§

Developmental progression in spelling follows the stages of development described in Chapter 2 (see Figure 1 on page 14). Children move from almost total reliance on simplistic sound-symbol relations in the Phonetic Stage. Word knowledge becomes increasingly complex to include such sound patterns as digraphs, diphthongs, and blends in the Graphophonic Stage. Letter patterns that do not have a good sound match but are more visual and word-knowledge patterns begin to be evident in the Orthographic Stage. Finally, meaning-based cues are incorporated as children move into the Morphophonic Stage. These include letter clusters, such as *re* or *psych* or *ing*, that convey meaning. Transition through these stages is never linear or sequential and is context dependent. This means that the grade levels assigned in Figure 3 are approximations. Actual application will depend on the individual groups of students.

A blank copy of the Expected Learning Outcomes chart (Figure 3) has been included in Black Line Master (BLM) 1 in the back of this book. This may serve as an assignment checklist for the class to be used in the same manner as the Class Spelling Profile, BLM 2, or as a tracking record of when specific skills were introduced.

Factors That Influence Spelling Success

Successful spelling is the result of the coordination of attitude, self-perception, thought processes, behaviors, and word knowledge. We can provide explicit instruction in word knowledge and strategic processes. Attitude and conceptual development about how to spell effectively are less straightforward, but equally important. The latter often develop as a result of the classroom environment and nonverbal messages we present. The conditions listed below reflect essential concepts about spelling that facilitate success.

Attitude and Confidence

A positive, effortful attitude and the confidence to take risks is essential to spelling competence. Long-term changes are dependent on specific strategy knowledge, self-monitoring, and motivation (Borkowski et al., 1992). Motivation, which is determined by one's confidence and attitude, is a significant variable in facilitating success (Scott, Hiebert, & Anderson, 1992). If our attitude as teachers demonstrates overtly that diversity and individual thinking are valued, then we promote long-term success. Mistakes must be viewed as an essential part of development and as something that everyone makes. A belief that spelling requires thought and effort and that it is important is also crucial. Confidence and attitude should be discussed openly with children. The most effective guidance comes from modeling attitudes we want to encourage.

Metacognition

Metacognition has been defined as both the awareness of a variety of strategies and the ability to select the most likely strategy and then monitor its effectiveness (Palincsar & Ransom, 1988). It is knowing what to do when you don't know what to do, that is, knowing what to do to set about spelling an unknown word. The more we can help children take control of their learning, the more successful and independent we make them (Wade & Reynolds, 1989). To develop metacognition, children need opportunities to talk and think about their spelling strategies. Metacognitive reflection should be an integral part of the spelling program.

Cueing Systems

The senses (visual, auditory, kinesthetic, and tactile) provide cues or prompts to help the brain store or access items in memory. Depending on past experience and individual learning style, strategies using the different senses may be more or less developed and effectively used for spelling. Children who have difficulty spelling often seem to be overreliant on a cueing system, most often using the auditory strategy of *sound it out*, although they usually have had little instruction in how to use even this cueing system effectively. Children who have not learned to use all the various cueing systems will benefit from specific instruction. Hearing discussion and suggestions from others will provide the awareness and language necessary to become better at application.

Visual cueing. Visual encoding and retrieval can be a useful spelling strategy (Tarasoff, 1990). As noted earlier, good spellers are able to determine whether a word looks right and to remember how the word looks from their reading. In school, visualization often is a technique used almost exclusively in primary grades and less in the intermediate and secondary grades, yet many adults admit that this is the way they find and fix mistakes. Research has shown that words retain a visual link even when the auditory link is lost (Templeton, 1986) For example, *sign* is linked to *signature* more visually than auditorally. Direct instruction in recalling where the word was seen, in learning to "see" letters, and in creating visual images may be beneficial.

Auditory cueing. Patterning or rhythm can be a useful memory clue. This strategy involves using rhythm and intonation while spelling words aloud and writing them. It has been used effectively in many traditional spelling strategies (Graham & Miller, 1979), and it has been found that many children prefer the auditory mode (Yong & McIntyre, 1992). Some instruction in use of this method of learning may prove beneficial for students because effective use or even awareness of the value of auditory cueing may not come naturally. One component of auditory cueing that is not always readily apparent to parents and teachers is phonemic awareness. Some children may require help in learning how to segment or say a word slowly enough to distinguish individual phonemes (Lie, 1991; Yopp, 1992). Although some sounds may be distorted, rendering this strategy less effective, it has been found that instruction in this area can be helpful (Ball & Blackman, 1991).

Tactile and kinesthetic cueing. The sense of touch and movement establish motor patterns that stimulate memory. Motor patterns are generated as students write and say the letter sequences for spelling words. Many students need instruction in using this sensory system to their advantage. Explain to them that writing a difficult word as it is spelled aloud will help build a tactile memory of the word that will supplement the auditory one created by saying the letters. It also produces a visible form (visual memory) that can be proofread. This is not to suggest that "writing out words *n* times" is a useful learning strategy, as it removes the words from a meaningful writing context. The less relevant an activity seems, the less likely retention will occur.

Mnemonic Strategies

Memory devices are sometimes the only way students remember the spelling of difficult or unusual words. We can teach children how to create them and when to use them. Most of the traditional methods used to learn the spelling of words are mnemonic strategies. These include *See, Cover, Spell, Check* (Graham & Miller, 1979) or creating acronyms or jingles to prompt memory (Tarasoff, 1990). For example, I remember there are two *S*'s in *dessert* and not in *desert* because I want two helpings.

Graphophonic Strategies

The controversy surrounding phonics comes with *how* we teach phonics, not *whether* we teach it (Stahl, 1992). Guiding children to make their own, personal interpretations of the sound-symbol relations in our language is much more effective than having them memorize rules. For example, in a sort-and-classify activity using words with a *ik* sound, groups of students were able to devise and share with the class their own perfectly valid rules for when to use *ic* or *ick* to write the sound. This was more powerful than me telling them my rule. They are much more likely to remember their own interpretation.

As noted earlier, good spellers use a variety of strategies. Poor spellers often are able to identify only one—most often *sound it out*—and they make no attempt to supplement phonics with semantic or syntactic information. They are overreliant on phonics, although it may not necessarily suit their learning profile. Very often children need guidance in effectively using this process—such as how to stretch words to hear the individual sounds or how to break words into only the necessary parts rather than all the individual sounds. It is necessary to supplement phonics with other strategies and not to succumb to the automatic reaction of giving them an intensive, remedial phonics program (Personke & Yee, 1971).

Outside Sources

External aides such as dictionaries or textbooks, and experts like teachers, parents, or even peers are valid sources of information. Even good spellers check with a friend or other expert at times, and all writers should know how to use a dictionary to look up unknown words. Do not assume children know how to use this resource effectively. Direct instruction is important.

Proofreading

Although students need to know when to rely on outside help, the ultimate goal of a spelling program is for students to be able to self-monitor personal writing. Our goal is to facilitate independent, autonomous learners, not ones who are reliant on the teacher for monitoring and gauging success (Weinstein, 1987). Identifying, teaching, and giving students practice in effective proofreading strategies will take the secrecy out of the process and facilitate competence.

Homonyms

Homonyms are the source of the greatest number of spelling errors in intermediate grades and, therefore, should be the focus of direct instruction (Thomas, 1979). Students usually need awareness and guidance in identifying these tricky words and strategies for remembering them.

Morphographs

Morphographs are the smallest letter clusters that retain meaning (suffixes, prefixes, and inflectional endings). Children are often amazed when they discover that if they know one word, they are actually able to spell many words (Templeton, 1979). We cannot assume children automatically grasp this concept. Simon and Simon (1973) suggested that we must teach children to attend to parts of words because this information is often not learned sufficiently simply through reading.

Studying Word Origins and Meaning

Understanding the origins of words can also help clarify the spelling process and enable children to make more reasonable attempts. As noted in the discussion on visualization earlier, visual orthographic information is often more stable than phonetic information and words retain a link with meaning rather than with sound (Templeton, 1979). For example, *sign* looks like *signature* but does not sound like it. Helping students become aware of historical origins can not only generate interest and motivation but foster successful spelling based on meaning. It gives additional basis for a *generate-and-test* (Simon & Simon, 1973) approach that has been found to be most effective. Using this strategy, children generate their best guess for an unknown word and then check to see if it is correct. Word origins or meaning cues can give them a starting place for their best guess.

A Unique Approach to Spelling Instruction

The Spelling Book was designed to form a daily part of the writing program. Direct instruction not only ensures that necessary information is shared, but it reinforces that spelling is important and worthy of care and attention. Although flexibility is important, making spelling a visible part of the schedule reinforces this attitude.

Because of the fundamental philosophical underpinnings of this book, the basic components of the program differ from the pretest, word-study activities, posttest sequence found in most traditional spelling programs. Ongoing, continuous study and analysis of words as they come up in daily language activities is the vehicle for constant refinement and deepening understanding. Regurgitation of the teacher's version of spelling structures is replaced by individual interpretation that is linked to personal experience and understanding. Such scaffolding requires interactive learning strategies that encourage independent thinking.

General Management Strategies

Teaching and management strategies, which effectively create these bridges, are those that help students understand the thinking processes used by expert spellers and provide opportunities for clarifying personal understanding. Reflective logs (rather than exercise books), partner spelling "tests," and personal dictionaries are some of the techniques that encourage students to extend their thinking and make connections. Rather than imparting information, teachers encourage observation and awareness. Some management and basic learning tools central to this instructional methodology are described in this chapter.

Responsive Planning

Lessons should be planned to meet observed needs. Group lessons may be an effective vehicle for determining future lessons. For example, group proofreading of a volunteered story may reveal misconceptions about when to use *ick* and when to use *ic*. The teacher then can structure a lesson at a later date that ensures that the children at least are exposed to the information. Not all of the class will remember or use the information at this time, any more than they would all remember and use a phonics rule presented for memorization. Those who are ready for it will internalize it, but those who are not may recall it when presented with it later in a different context. Because most lessons do not present isolated skills, the rationale and personal interpretation for rules are constantly being shared by students, and frequent repetition is inevitable.

Assessment and evaluation must be comprehensive and broad based. Little value is placed on scores, but the insights gained from misspelling analysis are invaluable in making program decisions. Information is gathered from a variety of sources and is used for analysis to determine both word knowledge and metacognitive levels. Chapter 5 gives more detailed information on ongoing assessment and evaluation.

Class Profile. In order to structure activities to meet identified need rather than a preset sequence, it is helpful to identify individual areas of need in one place. The Class Profile is a format for planning lessons around individual assessment. BLM 2 provides grids designed to assist in planning lessons. It is not the intention of this program to try to implement 27 individual spelling programs, but to help in planning activities that will help all children to continue to progress in their spelling development. The grid is used as a checklist to record the results of formal and informal assessment. Student names are listed along the side. A mark is placed in the column under the skill-strategy area in which a weakness has been noted. For example, if Belinda makes very little effort to spell even basic vocabulary, a check might be placed in the *attitude* column beside her name. If it seems apparent that Navie is ready for instruction in suffixes, then a mark would be put in the *affixes* column. When the grid is completed, the overview it gives of the class's needs makes selecting and planning lessons much more purposeful.

Attitude

Spelling lessons should encourage the attitudes we want children to adopt. Promoting a sense of discovery and of fun will go a long way in motivating children to learn to spell. There should be lots of smiles and "aha's." The attitude children bring to their spelling determines their success, and we determine that attitude by what we model in our teaching. Children need to recognize the following:

- *Shared thinking is valuable*, it is not cheating. Watching others, listening to their thinking, and sharing ideas are all important learning experiences that all learners, even adults, engage in. Much of what we know has been learned by modeling others;
- *Diverse opinions are valuable*, because there is always more than one way to think about things; and
- *Mistakes are a natural part of learning*. Experimentation with the language is the most effective way to become a good speller and is the way to test hypotheses about rules or individual words.

Teachers should model a positive attitude during both group and individual lessons.

Spelling Lessons

Along with strategies to spell words correctly, children need opportunities to continue to develop their awareness, knowledge, and personal understanding of orthography, the structures, relations, and rules on which the correct spelling of our language is based. It is not enough to leave this growth to chance.

Although many of the rules of our language are inconsistent, some do have a high reliability. It is important that children have repeated and varied experiences in working with these patterns so that they can form their own generalizations. The teacher's task is to plan the exposure thoughtfully and guide strategic thinking through questioning and prompts during daily word-study lessons. Lessons refer here to teaching situations that are deliberately structured to ensure that children observe and become aware of spelling structures. Complete descriptions of sample lessons are given in Chapter 7, and Figure 4 provides a list of the lesson plans and the skills they address.

All lessons in *The Spelling Book* are designed to provide opportunities for student-created generalizations about rules or common orthographic structures using theme-related literature or samples of draft writing from volunteers, and to provide opportunities to play with, manipulate, and explore words and spelling.

Figure 4 Lesson Goals

	Attitude	Metacognition	Visual Strategies	Phonics	Affixes	Homophones	Derivatives	Frequent Words	Unused Words	Proofreading
ABC Order Cards			•					•	•	
Building Blocks	•	•	•	•	•		•	•		•
Carousel Brainstorm	•	•		•	•					
Check It Out	•		•	•	•	•	•	•	•	•
Cluster Collection	•	•	•	•	•			•		
Cluster Relay			•	•	•		•	•		
Derivatives Cloze	•	•	•				•	•	•	
Endings Cloze	•	•	•		•		•	•		
Endings Reflection	•	•	•		•		•	•		
Error Data Collection	•	•	•	•	•	•	•	•	•	•
Find Some	•	•	•	•	•	•	•	•	•	•
Flower Power	•			•			•	•		•
Frequent Word List	•	•						•		
Guess My Thinking	•	•	•	•	•	•	•	•	•	•
Hilarious Homonyms	•	•	•			•				
Homonym Cloze	•	•	•			•				
Homonym Mnemonic	•	•				•				
Homonym Sort	•	•	•			•				
ICE	•	•	•		•			•	•	•
Impromptu "Test"			•	•				•		
Letter Clusters	•	•	•	•	•			•		
Letter Ladder			•	•				•		
Link-up Lists			•	•		•	•			
List Cloze			•	•	•		•	•	•	•
Looking Good	•	•	•				•	•	•	•
Make a Rule	•	•		•	•	•	•			
Make Words			•	•	•		•	•		
Making Meaning	•	•	•						•	
Marking Guide	•	•	•	•	•	•	•	•	•	•
Parents as Partners	•	•	•	•	•	•	•	•	•	•
Proofreading	•	•	•	•	•	•	•	•	•	•
Questionnaires	•	•								
Rap	•	•						•	•	
Setting the Stage	•	•						•		
SIP	•	•	•	•	•		•	•	•	•
Spelling Logs	•	•	•	•	•	•	•	•	•	•
Student Teacher	•	•	•	•	•	•	•	•	•	
That Reminds Me	•	•	•		•	•	•			•
Think of a Time	•	•								
What's in a Name?	•	•			•		•		•	
Word Banks	•	•	•		•	•		•	•	•
Write a Picture	•	•	•		•		•			
Writer's Report Card	•	•	•	•	•	•	•	•	•	•

These lessons provide an outline that may be followed initially. As the lessons are applied, they will be changed and adapted to individual teacher style and classroom situation. There is not one right way or sequence to use these plans. Different teachers, different students, different places, and different themes all mean different methods.

Children should engage in purposeful spelling activities daily. The focus and format of the instructional activities will be selected on the basis of identified need and the classroom context. For example, if assessment has identified a need for instruction in homophones or high-frequency words, a lesson on one of these topics from Chapter 7 can be selected to fit with the current classroom areas of study, such as science or a novel study, so the instruction can be contextually based.

The planned lessons frequently begin with a whole-group activity or focused discussion followed by guided practice in small cooperative groups. Individual application is monitored in independent cross-curricular writing. Both planned and informal instruction to address individual needs occur during minilessons which can take place during writing conferences or group lessons.

The only rule about the lessons is—stick to teaching kids to spell, not to memorize!

The unique feature of the lessons presented in this program is that they are never based on a predetermined list of words that the children memorize. Word lists that at times may be used are only for word-study activities. Most often the lists used contain words that have been brainstormed by the children, possibly for thematic work. They also may be examples of a particular spelling structure, or be prompted by an example found in a group proofreading activity. At times, the teacher may present a list of words for the children to play with to discover or practice a spelling structure, but the children are not expected to learn the whole words. As much as possible the words come from the context of the children's study or independent writing.

Whole-Group Lessons

Many of the lessons reflect at least in part a whole-group format. The students may be seated at their desks, in rows, in pods, or in a group, and an overhead projector may be used. Because the object of this program is immersion more than specific isolated skills, the whole-group format that facilitates repetition, observation, and discussion is used often. The real challenge of whole-group lessons is ensuring active participation by all students. It is usually the students who need the information the most who tune out. Lessons are structured to encourage maximum participation from all students, although challenged learners may need extra prompts or support to practice and internalize the concepts. If we can make the lessons interesting and nonthreatening, with settings where all ideas and opinions are valued, the poor speller is much more likely to participate and share his or her thinking. Examples of this kind of encouragement are, Which spelling would you use Trevor? or Have you ever noticed a word that uses that rule?

Guided thinking. Whole-group lessons allow the teacher to structure and guide the lesson to ensure the children become aware of the desired focus. For example, if the teacher has identified a general need for information on contractions, a lesson is chosen or developed to ensure the class observes and learns about them. This may involve a piece of student writing containing contractions or a cloze passage in which contractions have been blanked out. Shared thinking is encouraged and facilitated. Clarification may be provided or misconceptions discussed. At this time the teacher is able to model appropriate language for describing the spelling strategies, to highlight or paraphrase thinking shared by student volunteers, and to monitor participation. Whenever possible, follow-up includes direct application to individual writing—such as finding examples of the targeted structure in their own story.

Cooperative Learning

Cooperative learning is an instructional technique in which students are placed in small groups for the purpose of learning something new or completing a task. The group works collaboratively, with each member contributing to overall success in a meaningful way. The sense of camaraderie and belonging that is developed through members supporting and learning from one another enhances learning. The tasks and groups are structured by the teacher to promote this positive interdependence. Many of the lessons used in this program are based on a cooperative learning format. There are several reasons for this philosophy. Cooperative learning has been shown to be effective (Slavin, 1987; Villa & Thousand, 1988) in achieving both group and individual goals. It prompts higher-order thinking rather than just rote memory because discussion and debate are encouraged and facilitated. Children are motivated to help one another, and they do not just give answers, they explain their responses. Cooperative groups can provide effective instruction in a very supportive environment. Students work with their friends, which allows them to take risks and gain confidence. A young, very challenged speller commented one day about a cooperative group activity, "I realized that other people make mistakes too." What a wonderful discovery for a child with low self-confidence!

Structured discussion. One of the most valuable aspects of cooperative learning is that it can be structured to promote discussion. Discussion, including shared thinking and verbalized learning, is the most powerful way to learn (Slavin, 1987). It is no secret that active engagement with material being studied will help to develop a more personal and thorough understanding of the concept being presented than just trying to memorize the teacher's interpretation or rules. When children are able to explain new learning in their own words, they have internalized their understanding and demonstrated their comprehension.

Group size. The size of the group should reflect the goals of the lesson. If a group brainstorm is required, a group of six students is workable, but for powerful shared thinking and written work, I have found partnerships or triads to be most effective. Activities such as sorting and classifying have a number of steps involved and work best with lots of shared ideas for sorting. Groups of four work well for these.

Group participation. To ensure full and equal group participation, I stress three group rules:

> *Call on the less-able student first, before someone else takes his or her good idea. This builds confidence by allowing the student to give the more obvious answer and invites successful participation.*

- Everyone must participate.
- Everyone must cooperate.
- Everyone must know the answer, that is, anyone in the group that is called on should be able to explain the group's thinking and rationalization.

These rules are restated at the beginning of each activity.

Assignment of specific jobs is a good method of keeping everyone involved and doing their share. The jobs will vary, but some suggestions follow:

Manager or Chairperson. This student makes sure everyone is on task, the job is completed, and disputes are settled. He or she also encourages participation.

Equipment Manager. This student gets, keeps track of, and returns equipment.

Secretary. This student is responsible for making sure the writing is done. This may be done alone or may be a shared task.

Reporter or Speaker. This student orally presents the group findings during sharing time.

Time Keeper. As the name indicates, this student watches the clock.

Other specific tasks, such as *Gluer* or *Cutter* may be designated as well, depending on the task. The only task that may not be allocated to a single individual is that of Thinker.

Group skills take time to build, but are worth the effort. I have yet to find a more effective way to encourage full participation and involvement or to model that acceptance and value of everyone's ideas.

Five-Minute Sessions

Spelling lessons do not have to be extended or in depth to be worthwhile. In fact, some of the most beneficial and memorable spelling experiences may come from frequent, quick, off-the-cuff opportunities to observe, confirm, or verbalize spelling structures or strategies. Short forays into spelling that occur while engaged in another subject effectively reinforce transfer and application of knowledge gained during a structured spelling time. They provide time for practice and reinforcement of rules and observations or to reinforce consistency and build an attitude of importance.

Teachable moments may present themselves through any activity involving the use of written language. For example, group reading of a social studies passage may reveal an example of a previously highlighted rule. ("Oh look, there's that *ous* ending again!") Focusing attention takes about 30 seconds and goes a long way in reinforcing application in a naturalistic, pragmatic context. ("Did you notice that *industrialized* is spelled like *industry*? It would fit on the list we made the other day. Let's see if there are any others.") Encouraging students to acknowledge such tangents keeps spelling within the realm of real writing and encourages extended thinking and application beyond the spelling lesson. Detailed descriptions of further examples of quick practice sessions or 5-minute spelling lessons are provided in Chapter 7.

Spelling Tools

The Spelling Tools used in this book include instructional strategies such as Spelling Logs, personal dictionaries called Word Banks, and weekly Spelling "Tests." These elements of the program give it a framework or structure, much like the texts or workbooks found in other programs.

Spelling Logs are notebooks that will be used continuously. Students use them like workbooks for word-study activities or assignments, as "think paper" to try out ideas or jot down lists or words during discussions, and as journals to record new understandings and reflections. Similarly, Word Banks are booklets students create that house each student's list of important words. They will be used frequently during class writing and during spelling tests. Weekly Spelling "Tests" are another constant feature of this program. Children engage in a spelling test weekly, however it is not one for which they can study because the goal is not to memorize a list of words.

Spelling Tools are important because they provide an organizational framework for teaching and learning. The structure is similar to workbooks or exercise books, but the Tools have a very different connotation. Because they are not restricted to production of the correct response, they invite and encourage active, risk-free language study. Rather than trying to guess the teacher's answer or the standard spelling, children come to understand that their own ideas and questions are important, that being able to put ideas into their own words is meaningful, that it is okay to try out things, and that learning is often not neat and sequential but random and messy.

Spelling Logs

Spelling Logs are reflective journals or notebooks in which students record, in their own words, their observations and increasing understanding of English spelling. You can use Spelling Logs to record each child's learning, reflections, and observations and to facilitate metacognition for word-study activities.

For example, following a lesson on homonyms, students might be directed to write in their own words their understanding of the key points to remember about the words they studied. Or perhaps after a generic spelling strategy has been introduced, students might record when, where, or how the strategy might be applied or how they might teach it to a younger student. During an activity in which groups are exploring word origins, a list of words might need to be written. Perhaps two or three attempts at a word might need to be jotted down to determine which one looks right. Spelling Logs provide appropriate think paper for this activity. Figure 5 on page 36 provides a list of prompts you can use to start students writing in their Spelling Logs.

The emphasis when using Spelling Logs is on the students recording their own understandings of a concept, not echoing the teacher's rule or interpretation. Because Spelling Logs are journals and not exercise books, the focus is not on the right answer, but rather on thinking, reflection, and documentation of personal understandings.

These books are not marked in a traditional manner, but are useful for teacher assessment and evaluation. The recordings found therein give au-

Figure 5 Spelling Log Prompts

I used the think _____, but now I know _____.

I was surprised to learn that _____.

I didn't realize that _____. It makes sense now because _____.

Something I learned today that I will be able to use again is _____.

This strategy will be useful when I'm _____.

How would you teach this strategy to another person?

What "big" words do you think you will be able to spell now?

Do the examples we saw today make you think of any others?

What is the most important thing to remember about this strategy?

Explain this (strategy/activity/discussion topic) in your own words.

thentic evidence of topic comprehension. The entries are not necessarily right or wrong; they simply give the teacher information about the current thinking. There is no point in *marking* a reflection, but there is value in using the information to structure a minilesson as needed to clarify a misconception. Spelling Logs provide a cumulative record of each child's developmental perceptions about phonics, grammar, structural analysis, and homonyms, which is readily available for assessment.

Remember that entries are made in the student's own words. They may be in response to directed prompts or completed in a free-write format, but students should feel confident to record their own thoughts without fear of repercussion. They should, however, recognize the importance of the journals and not view them as just something to be gotten out of the way. It is perfectly acceptable to encourage and require thoughtful, comprehensive entries. This helps to reinforce the importance of spelling while respecting students' personal interpretations. Entries may be made before, during, or after lessons, activities, or discussions and should be made at least two or three times per week.

Word Banks

Word Banks are personal dictionaries used within the writing process. Each child creates an alphabetized list of words that they may refer to when writing. Word Banks may also be used to provide words for dictation on spelling tests.

Word Banks are an extremely useful tool that

- provide a personal dictionary for use in independent writing;
- provide an opportunity to write correct spelling, thus creating a mental image of the correct spelling of the word;
- develop an attitude that correct spelling is important;
- provide an effective, simple means of locating needed words;

- provide an opportunity to highlight and focus key letter sequences of new words;
- provide motivation because words are self-selected; and
- provide a list of words to use for spelling tests.

To develop and use Word Banks create a "dictionary." Small notebooks work well; format each one with one letter on each double page. This may be done by you or by the student. Students usually enjoy creating a title page and personalizing the book. Model how to record the first 5–10 words. This process sets the tone for future use and emphasizes the purpose for putting words in the Word Bank. This purpose is to be able to find them and use them and to assist in remembering them.

Accuracy is vital in Word Banks, and so is choosing the best strategy to find the spelling and record it. Asking an expert or using the dictionary are good choices, but sounding out a word is not acceptable because it may not give correct spelling. Correct spelling *must* be stressed and monitored by the teacher for the first few weeks. If the teacher provides the word, it should be printed on the board or another piece of paper for the student to copy. Although it seems like more work, this is of great benefit to the student. It provides the correct visual stimulus that is reinforced by the physical act of copying. Saying the letters out loud provides an auditory stimulus.

Words in the Word Bank should be printed in list form as this facilitates visual analysis and organization. It is much easier to find words in a list.

Introducing Word Banks. Tell the students about the book and its purpose, then select a word and write it on the board. The students write the word on the appropriate alphabet page in their Word Bank. You should discuss the fact that it is essential that the word is spelled correctly. Tell students a dictionary must be used or that they should ask you for the spelling. After the word is entered, it is useful to mark a clue in the word with a colored pencil (for example, a cluster, vowel or consonant combination, or affix). This provides a reinforcing visual clue. Model this process:

> The word is *picnic*. *Ic* is unusual. It is often *ick*. I also want to remind myself that there are 2 *ic*'s in this word, so I'll use my highlighter to mark them. That will help me remember them.

When students are familiar with the process, they should choose 10–20 words that are important to them for entry in their Word Bank. They should be encouraged to share their words and the clues that they marked. Following initial introduction and instruction, new words are recorded during independent writing activities.

Word Banks should form an integral part of the writing program and should be referred to frequently so children develop a habit of using them. During independent writing or any time a student asks for the spelling of a word, the new word should be recorded in the Word Bank. Students should be encouraged to look in their Word Bank before requesting assistance because the words recorded there are words that the student is currently using in their personal writing and studies and are always therefore developmentally appropriate.

Because the words recorded in the Word Banks are personally selected by the student as being of interest or as part of his or her high-frequency list, they are naturally relevant and appropriate for dictation. The author has indicated by recording them that they are worth thinking about and remembering.

Weekly Spelling "Tests"

Although called weekly "tests," these activities are really just structured opportunities for students to practice applying spelling strategies and monitoring their growth in spelling. They are informal, self-monitored tests in which partners dictate words to each other. Because words for dictation are chosen by a partner at random, no opportunity is provided to prestudy. The goal is practice, not memorization. Students mark their own test, correct errors, and record their success on a graph. These "tests" do not form part of the teacher's formal assessment, although they do provide considerable information for planning instruction.

Introducing spelling "tests." Dictation Books may be made by stapling 10–20 copies of BLM 3 into a booklet. A graph may be included at the back of the Dictation Book on which is recorded the weekly score. This graph is used for student monitoring only, and is not used for teacher evaluation or spelling marks.

Working with partners, students participate in a spelling "test" once a week (usually Friday) using words from their personal Word Banks. Word Banks are exchanged and partners decide who will dictate first. Ten words are selected by one student and dictated to the other. The words are chosen at random by the first student. It is not desirable for students to study for this test. The second student writes words as they are dictated, without comment from the reader. No help or correcting from the partner is allowed.

As the words are being dictated, the teacher is available to read any unknown word a partner may encounter. This happens often because the words belong to the "test" taker, and it is acceptable for the reader not to know them or to be unable to read the handwriting. Nonchalant support by the teacher gives challenged spellers the confidence to participate actively. When the "test" taker has finished, student roles are reversed.

Following dictation, each child marks his or her own test, comparing the words he or she wrote to those in the Word Bank and then recording his or her own score. A graph showing the number or words spelled correctly from week to week encourages self-competition. See Figure 6 for more examples of dictation techniques.

The "test" session should always be followed by group discussion focusing on successes and errors, strategies used, and things to remember in the future. Questions asked can include: What word do you feel proud of? How did you figure it out? Reflections on the "tests" should be recorded 2–3 times per month in Spelling Logs during a 5-minute write.

Teachers are often concerned about students cheating on this type of test. However, because the goal is a structured time for students to think about spelling, whether by looking up the word, asking someone, or even changing their answer, cheating is not a concern. Students are accomplishing the task because they have to think about and visualize the spelling in order to change an answer. These "tests" are not used for marks or evaluating student progress, so cheating really does not matter, and deemphasizing scores miraculously diminishes incidences.

Figure 6 Options for Dictation

1. A list of high-frequency words may be printed in alphabetic clusters and pasted in the Word Bank. The importance of remembering these words has already been discussed in class. (A rule may be made that a specified number of the dictated words must be from these high-frequency words.)

2. Have the dictator put a mark beside the dictated words. This helps to avoid constant repetition.

3. Have the author put a mark beside ones that he or she is able to consistently spell correctly so they are not repeated.

4. Have partners discuss before the test whether they want an easy, medium, or challenging day. Students get bored if the words are too easy.

Error analysis. Error analysis is a process of self-evaluation in which students gradually become aware of common error types or patterns. The goal of this activity is for students to become able to describe their types of errors and set an area of focus. The types of errors children make are relatively few. Self-evaluation of error types can lead to increased awareness and attention. Several activities are suggested in Chapter 7 to introduce error analysis and provide practice. Once the children have gained some competence in this area, they may begin to analyze their test performance. The analysis may be recorded on the dictation sheets.

Two examples of Spelling Dictation black line masters are provided in BLM 3. One suggests error categories, the other is blank. With some classes, you may prefer to use the category labels that you devise during activities.

High-Frequency Words

These words are worth remembering. They are words that research has shown to have a high occurrence in children's writing. These are the words that most spelling programs have been built upon, because they are what children most need to develop automatically to achieve fluency. Ironically they also contain a high percentage of *demon words*, or words that do not follow the rules.

Most spelling programs and many researchers have published lists of high-frequency words (Scott & Siamon, 1994; Thomas & Braun, 1979). The lists are not all identical because there are many factors affecting how often a word is used—age, experience, geographic location, and year—but consistency is not important because really it is the concept that matters, not the words themselves. We need to help children realize that some words are used so often it is best to remember how to spell them than to try to figure them out anew each time they are encountered. Children need to understand that many of these words have irregular spellings and that the sound-it-out strategy does not work well in spelling them. They need to develop a spelling conscience about these words, to understand that it is important to spell them correctly.

The Spelling Book deals with high-frequency words in several ways. Honest, open discussion about the concept is suggested in Chapter 6, as is creating

As students are introduced to this type of "test," open discussion should occur about words being either too hard or too easy. Because of the low-risk setting, students generally agree that having all easy words is boring. There is no satisfaction if there is no challenge, although it is perfectly acceptable to have an off day occasionally and want only easy words. Giving students the opportunity to make a choice of easy or difficult words and to let their partner know what kind of words to dictate really seems to facilitate motivation. I was initially surprised to find even poor spellers complain that the words were too easy.

personal or class high-frequency word lists rather than using prepublished ones. High-frequency words should be included when introducing the generic spelling strategies in Chapter 4, and several word-study lessons using them are presented in Chapter 7. Suggestions for ways parents can teach them have been given in Chapter 8.

Scheduling Spelling

I found it helpful to schedule my lessons in the weekly timetable. Spelling ideally should not need to be scheduled but should be an extension of the writing program (Gentry, 1987; Henderson, 1981) with brief lessons, as appropriate and within pragmatic writing, reflecting current need. However, in reality I was not always quite that organized. With the time demands of the classroom and the busy schedule, spelling tended to get replaced if it was not written into my schedule! I included spelling for 15–20 minutes per day. This time was very flexible, but at least if I scheduled it there was more chance to retain continuity.

The most successful place I found to schedule spelling was during times when the class would be doing independent writing—creative writing, any language arts activity, or adjacent to content subjects such as social studies or science. Scheduling spelling at times of entry, such as first thing in the morning or afternoon or just after recess, has also been effective in many classrooms. It seems less easily interrupted and forgotten at these times. See Figure 7 for sample weeks of spelling schedules.

Lessons will look different with each different focus. They may be extended word-study activities that complement and extend thematic study, or they may be short, lasting just 5–10 minutes. Suggestions for both will be described.

Be prepared to be flexible. Although an average of 15–20 minutes per day is suggested, some lessons may be longer. Formal lessons may occur only once or twice in a week. Devoting larger blocks of time less often provides a welcome variety, however it should not occur frequently. Consistency and continuity are key ingredients to steady progress.

Note that the lesson on Monday often influences the lessons that occur during the rest of the week. Whole-group activities are excellent means to assess misconceptions, and the observant teacher will structure lessons that draw out student knowledge and plan subsequent lessons accordingly. Connections among lessons support effective learning and transfer. In addition, students should have many opportunities scheduled during which they are actively proofreading their own writing. Because in a busy classroom it is sometimes difficult to ensure that children put words into their Word Bank as they come up during writing, it is helpful to schedule a Word Bank period every week or two. This not only provides words for Spelling "Tests," but also provides a growing list of words that students should be encouraged to consult as they are engaged in independent writing.

For those times when there are interruptions to the regular schedule, spelling activities should reflect the theme and fit around the events. These

Figure 7 Sample Weeks of Spelling Lessons

	Monday	Tuesday	Wednesday	Thursday	Friday
Week 1	Whole-Group Cloze (15 minutes) misconceptions about contractions noted	Coop Group Find & Fix (25 minutes) group proofreading focusing on contractions	Complete sharing from Tuesday Debrief Spelling Log entry (20 minutes)	Enter words into Word Bank and share (20 minutes)	Spelling "Test" (20 minutes)
Week 2	What's In A Name? (30 minutes) sort words into groups	Reflection Sheet— What's In A Name? (15 minutes)	Student Teacher (15 minutes) practice spelling using word origins	Word Relay (5 minutes just before recess)	Spelling "Test" (20 minutes)
Week 3	Whole-Group Proofread (15 minutes) find errors and share strategies for fixing	Partner Proofread (20 minutes) work on current piece of writing	Continue Proof-reading (15–20 minutes)	Debrief Share what was learned in proofreading and strategies used Spelling Log entry (15 minutes)	Spelling "Test" (20 minutes)
Week 4	Guess My Thinking (15 minutes) using errors from Friday test	Field Trip no spelling	Brainstorm/Categorize (30 minutes) using words brainstormed from trip, sort into groups by vowels	Share categories and rationales from Wednesday Record in Spelling Log (20 minutes)	Spelling "Test" (20 minutes)
Week 5	Independent Writing no formal spelling	Marking Sheet (25 minutes) Find and record errors on the sheet. Correct draft (words are put into Word Banks)	Look for patterns and Categorize errors Make suggestions (20 minutes)	Writer's Report Card (20 minutes)	Spelling "Test" (20 minutes)
Week 6		WINTER	CARNIVAL	WEEK	
	Sort Carnival word cards into ABC order (10 minutes)	Word Banks (20 minutes)	(classes disrupted) no formal spelling	Letter Ladder game (10 minutes)	Spelling "Test" (20 minutes) all Carnival words
Week 7	Whole-Group Cloze (10 minutes) social studies theme topic, endings	Flower Power (30 minutes) add endings to root words, proofread list	Complete Flower Power (30 minutes) present finished product and rationales	Debrief Record in Spelling Log (10 minutes)	Spelling "Test" (20 minutes)

Important Note

The weeks of spelling lessons described here could conceivably be the basis for several months of lessons. Because of the generic nature of the lessons, they are designed to be used over and over simply by plugging in different content or orthographic information. In fact, using the same lesson format is beneficial to students because as they gain familiarity they are able to spend more of their energy on learning and applying the spelling knowledge, rather than figuring out how to complete the exercise.

are times when short 5-minute activities are academically viable and are also a lifesaver in filling small amounts of time.

Conclusion

This chapter has presented an outline of the specific goals of spelling instruction, as well as a general description of management strategies, lesson formats, and tools you will use to implement this spelling methodology. These structures and tools provide the framework upon which to structure the spelling activities. A thoughtful, structured approach makes it easier to meet the goals than trusting that opportunities will just present themselves during writing events. The format described here makes it possible to have both structure and flexibility. Next I will discuss a series of generic spelling strategies that form the basis for instruction. These strategies are applicable in all writing contexts—independent writing, word-study activities, or even on a spelling "test." Spelling strategies are the tools that enable successful application of growing word knowledge.

4

Generic Spelling Strategies

Because we use them so automatically, we often do not think about the wide variety of strategies that help us to spell. We do not just sound out words or memorize them, the only strategies emphasized in traditional spelling programs. In talking to people about spelling, I always start by asking them to spell difficult words, *soliloquy* and *camaraderie*, and then ask them to reflect on how they attempted to spell the words. It is evident from this experiment that there is no one right way to spell that will be successful for all spellers, for all words, and in all writing situations. All good spellers use a variety of spelling strategies.

In Chapter 2, I identified the thinking processes used for spelling and described some aspects of effective teaching. As I also noted in Chapter 2, studies in cognitive psychology suggest that instruction should contain *strategic* elements as well as *content knowledge* (Wong, 1986). Through interviews with children, Radebaugh (1985) identified the strategies employed by good spellers, which include breaking words into parts, thinking about small words in big words, and monitoring whether the word looks right. A speller's confidence in his or her ability to spell new words was also identified as important to his or her success. Poor spellers reported using fewer strategies. They tended to spell letter by letter, seemed to be stuck in the phonetic stage of spelling, used few visual strategies, and showed little metacognition.

We know what good spellers do, and it makes sense to focus instruction on showing all students how to use these strategies. Spelling instruction should address three elements: instruction in how the language functions; instruction in strategies for applying the knowledge; and instruction in developing a confident, purposeful attitude (Paris, Lipson, & Wixon, 1983; Swanson, 1989; Wong, 1986). It is not enough to teach children about the rules and structure of English and assume they will apply the knowledge in their writing. Students also need direct guidance in applying these rules. Too often, successful spelling seems to be a mystery over which many students feel they have no control. The resulting negative or passive attitude leads to frustration and failure.

In this chapter the lessons focus on direct instruction in effective spelling strategies that may be used in *any* spelling situation, whether a personal letter, a report, or a formal spelling test. The balance of the book describes a methodology that has been designed to help children explore and develop an awareness of the structure of English and to provide direct teaching in using these generic spelling strategies to apply their growing content knowledge within the existing language arts program.

Teaching Generic Spelling Strategies

Children need to be aware of a variety of strategies to become competent spellers. It is the teacher's job to structure experiences that will ensure strategic development. Initial strategy awareness may develop through teacher modeling and be enhanced with group discussion, however direct instruction is often desirable to ensure that the student learns definite strategies. In the development of this program it became evident that distinct, recognizable strategies were easier to access and apply in writing than theoretical discussion. I found that if children could name and describe a strategy, they were much more likely to apply it. Such clarity also was seen to affect metacognition, which is the ability to discuss personal learning strategies. To meet this need, six spelling strategies were created, each with a memorable title. These are generic procedures that may be applied to any unknown word and they should be introduced through direct teaching. Techniques for teaching the strategies are given in this chapter and suggestions for guided practice through word-study activities are described in Chapter 7.

If children have not been previously exposed to spelling strategies they should be introduced gradually, but early in the year. It is not necessary for all the strategies to have been taught before engaging the children in the word-study activities as each provides a vehicle for practicing the other. Children are encouraged to think about and apply new spelling strategies to words as they work through activities that also are structured to increase their word knowledge. Such pragmatic application provides practice without using isolated exercises and is reinforced by using the teaching tools described in Chapter 3 such as Spelling Logs and Word Banks.

There is no particular order in which to teach the strategies presented in this chapter, except to consider that Building Blocks is most suitable for students in the later morphophonic stage of development. You therefore may find it most useful to introduce the other strategies first. Two strategies should be introduced fairly quickly. Providing the two options reinforces the desirability of selecting the method considered most appropriate for spelling a given word and monitoring its effectiveness. Children should be reasonably comfortable with each strategy before a new one is introduced. Competence can be judged by the their ability to describe the strategy, its application, and its benefits.

That Reminds Me...

Creating links between what children know already and new concepts is the key to successful learning. That Reminds Me... encourages children, through self-questioning, to relate the spelling of new words to known words with similar spelling patterns. Instead of simply memorizing rules, students are encouraged to think of how the rules have been applied in words they already know. This helps spelling make sense and enhances the chances of it being remembered.

Why use That Reminds Me...?	**Skill Development**
• It helps children apply, rather than just memorize spelling patterns.	• phonics
• It helps make spelling make sense by making connections.	• simple and complex letter clusters
• It can be used effectively in both visual and auditory spelling modes.	• suffixes and prefixes • origins and derivatives
• Children can make links to visual patterns they know or to words that sound the same.	• proofreading • mental dictionary
• It facilitates a positive and thoughtful attitude.	• metacognition

How to Introduce and Use That Reminds Me...

Awareness of connections among the spelling of words is essential for effective use of That Reminds Me.... This awareness is best developed through many experiences in sorting and classifying words by their letter clusters or sounds. Activities designed to provide this experience include Carousel Brainstorm (page 107), Cluster Relay (page 109), and Letter Ladder (page 109). Other activities in which generalizations are applied to many words also develop awareness and links. One such activity is Flower Power (page 107).

That Reminds Me... is a relatively simple strategy for students to use and is best introduced through direct instruction and mental modeling. Large group proofreading sessions or cloze lessons shown on an overhead are useful times to introduce the concept.

Model the use of self-questioning to link the unknown word to a known word, as in the following examples on the next page:

This reminds me of (a related word) because....

Is that like any word I already know?

Is there any other word that I know that looks or sounds the same?

Does it remind me of any other word?

After the process has been modeled many times, invite students to think aloud. As spellings are suggested, students are encouraged to share their thinking by giving their rationale for their spelling saying "That reminds me...."

Reflection in Spelling Logs should focus on putting into words how to use this strategy and why it will help a student be a better speller. Students also should identify when and where they will probably be able to use the strategy.

Looking Good

Looking Good is a strategy in which students are encouraged to inspect words visually. They are especially encouraged to look at unfamiliar words that they have spelled to check to see if they look right. For words that are spelled incorrectly or do not look right, one or more alternate spellings are generated. Through self-questioning, students learn to locate and alter only the part of the word with the suspected misspelling. Although at first it may seem that students have little capacity to use this strategy effectively, they usually improve significantly with practice. Looking Good is a strategy found to be particularly useful for frequently written words and is the basis for successful proofreading.

How to Introduce and Use Looking Good

Looking Good should be modeled many times by an adult, especially for poor spellers. This spelling strategy may be effectively introduced with the whole class during group proofreading activities but will need reinforcement during individual writing conferences.

Why use Looking Good?	Skill Development
• It helps students develop and access their visual memory.	• metacognition
• It encourages students to develop a spelling conscience—to check and monitor their accuracy.	• phonics
• It encourages children to be aware of the part of the word that may be wrong and to change only this part rather than starting the whole word over again.	• strategy for use with high-frequency words
• It helps spelling to make sense and therefore be predictable.	• proofreading
• It provides an effective strategy for applying word knowledge.	

It is important for children to recognize that misspelled words may be mostly right, with only a few letters incorrect. Introduce the strategy to the whole class by using an overhead projection of a student volunteer's writing. As the group reads through the story, identify a frequently used word that has been written incorrectly. Write the word in the margin three or four different ways, including the incorrect attempt, the correct way, and at least one other way, saying, "Think about the last time you saw the word. Let's see if we can find that spelling. Which one do you think looks right?" Have the children look carefully at the list and think of the times they have seen the word. They should then select the spelling that looks the most correct.

Many children, especially those for whom spelling is a challenge, will need frequent reinforcement and practice using this strategy. When working one-on-one with a student to help him or her identify correct spellings visually, he or she should have a Word Bank to locate the word and compare the spellings provided. The goal at this point is simply to have the student understand that correct spellings will often be recognized by the way they look.

BLM 4 may be useful in guiding an individual student's thinking through the Looking Good process. After a word from personal writing has been highlighted (either by the child or an adult) and written in the margin or on BLM 4, have the child decide what part of the word they are fairly certain is correct. He or she will usually be able to indicate at least the first or last letter or blend, and often he or she can identify more. Use questions to elicit suggestions from the child for other possible letters or clusters to try for the suspected errors: What else do you think we could try for this part? Write the word with the suggested changes in a list with the incorrect version. If the child is stuck, suggest parts of the word that might be changed:

What do you often see at the end of words?

What two letters often go together to make this part?

Is there another way to make that sound? What might it be?

You're missing a letter. What do you think it might be?

This is a funny word. Do you remember the letter that goes here?

Have the child attempt to choose the word that looks correct. Ask what prompted the choice. This gives the teacher insight into the thinking process being used and suggests areas for instruction. If the child makes a wrong choice, praise the attempt, give the correct word, and point out a part of the word to remember next time.

Although the goals of independent proofreading are to be able to locate errors and then to fix them, it is sometimes advantageous to break the task into manageable parts, especially if the student has many errors. To give practice specifically in using Looking Good, it is often helpful to circle the errors for the student so as not to overwhelm him or her. A computer spellchecker is also useful for this task. It will highlight the error and the student is then free to find the part to change.

Sound in Parts (SIP)

Sound in Parts (SIP) is a strategy that encourages children to break or segment words into their component parts to facilitate spelling. Many children do not automatically segment words into the more manageable syllables to facilitate spelling, although it is a strategy demonstrated by good spellers. SIP provides direct instruction in applying this strategy and is applicable to both auditory or visual analysis.

Why use SIP?	Skill Development
• It provides direct instruction and guided practice in breaking words into parts. • It provides opportunities to focus on common letter clusters and make generalizations. • It helps children effectively apply phonics knowledge. • It encourages confidence and independence. • It encourages metacognitive awareness that small parts are easier to spell and there are effective ways to use this knowledge.	• phonics • letter clusters • spelling strategy for use in all writing • metacognition

How to Introduce and Use SIP

As a class, discuss difficulties, frustrations, and successes in spelling longer words. Tell the students that they are going to learn a spelling strategy that will help to make those big words more manageable. Suggest that some words are just too big to tackle all at once and that it is easier to do a little bit at a time. Through clapping or intonation, introduce the concept of beats or sounds in words. Syllabication will not be a new concept for many of your students. Draw on that knowledge base by having these students share how they use this knowledge to help them spell. Other students, however, will still need a great deal of practice in simply saying words in parts. Their level of phonemic awareness will not be as developed. These students will need direct instruction and practice in pronouncing each segment carefully, or the spelling may be distorted.

After students have had practice and are familiar with the idea of breaking words into parts, introduce the concept of syllables as a useful strategy for spelling. Suggest the SIP acronym as a way to remember the strategy; for example, "Take little SIPs of big words." Continue to share many examples of how difficult words might be said in parts, but now model how to spell each individual part. Say and spell each individual part of the word. As suggestions for spelling word parts, draw attention to common letter clusters such as *tion* or *ight*:

va–ca ("How do I make shun?") tion

Once students are familiar with SIP, it is important to model the need for monitoring after the word is written: "That doesn't look right. That part sounded like *or*, but I remember it is *ar*." Provide many opportunities for the students to practice and encourage reflection in learning logs. Students should describe how to use the strategy in their own words and how they think it will help them become a better speller.

Rap

Rap may not be the best method for all spellers, but this auditory strategy can provide a useful method for some words, particularly unusual or trouble words. This strategy makes use of the popular genre of rap music, which relies heavily on beat and rhythm. The letter sequence of words is pronounced in a memorable rhythm or beat thus providing an auditory memory cue. Rap also encourages verbalization of letter sequence, which adds further sensory input and enhances memory. (I think most adults learned and still remember how to spell *Mississippi* by using Rap.)

Why use Rap?	Skill Development
• It encourages students to say letter sequences out loud, which prompts auditory memory. • It can be useful for high-frequency words as well as unusual words. • It provides a mnemonic strategy for long or hard words. • It provides a self-checking system, if children are encouraged to monitor accuracy.	• a strategy for difficult words • complex clusters

How to Introduce and Use Rap

To introduce this strategy, the children are invited to share their favorite rap songs and music. The ensuing discussion focuses on the beat and rhythm, which makes the songs memorable. Tell the students they are going to use this information to learn a strategy to remember how to spell some words, especially those that are long and cumbersome. An interesting fact to share is that poetry originated to help illiterate long-distance messengers around the time of the Roman Empire to remember their messages for a long time. Talk about how saying the letters in a rhythm or beat and saying the words out loud will stimulate their memory.

Students in groups of two or three are asked to prepare a rap show for the class. Each group selects a word they have decided is hard to spell and creates a song or rap in which the letters are presented in a rhythmic, memorable form. Each group performs their rap for the class, and the class then joins in and learns the rap.

Once students are familiar with the usefulness of rap, they can use it independently with words they feel they need to remember. Students are encouraged to verbalize the letters in rhythm as they are writing words (particularly in Word Banks, where the correct letter sequence is being written) and as they are attempting to spell the word in context. This stimulates auditory memory.

The value of looking at the word and reading the letters (aloud) should be discussed with the class and individuals to reinforce understanding and metacognition. When attempting to spell or check the accuracy of a troublesome word, this auditory memory can prove a valuable mnemonic prompt. Students also are encouraged to monitor their accuracy through self-questioning. Reading back the letters and asking "Does that sound right?" or "Does it look right?" will facilitate successful use. Personal understanding and reflections as to usefulness of this and all strategies should be recorded in Spelling Logs.

Imagine, Copy, Examine (ICE)

Imagine, Copy, Examine (ICE) is a spelling strategy that encourages the use of visual imagery and self-checking. Children try to recall seeing a needed word in their mind to help them remember the spelling. After the letters are written, the child examines them to see if they look as he or she recalled. The checking encourages self-monitoring.

Why use ICE?	Skill Development
• It provides an alternative for children who have trouble with the SIP strategy. • It provides a strategy for phonetically irregular words. • It actively stimulates visual memory. • It encourages self-monitoring.	• developing a spelling conscience and monitoring accuracy • simple and complex letter clusters • proofreading • high-frequency words

How to Introduce and Use ICE

For this strategy to be used most effectively with spelling, the children should have many experiences creating visual images of actual objects. Having them create images of food is a good way to start. When they have imagined a picture in their mind of breakfast, of something cold, or of something delicious, have them describe it in detail. What color is it? Describe the shape. Then have them recall and bring a picture to their mind of the last time they saw the word for the item.

Children then are encouraged to imagine a computer screen (or any other screen or board on which to place their word) in their mind. Choose a word that you are reasonably certain they will have seen recently. Ask them to think of the location in which they saw it, and ask volunteers to share the picture with the class. Where did they see the word? What does it look like? What kind of printing is it? Keeping the picture of the word in their mind, they are to type it onto the computer in their mind, which will reinforce the visual image. For extra practice, they can try to imagine the word in different sizes or different type styles.

The next step is to copy the word from the screen onto paper. The idea that it is copying rather than writing is emphasized at this time, to encourage children to retain the mental image rather than to just shut down the computer and write it from memory.

After the word is written on the paper, the students examine the word to see if it looks correct. Students are to ask themselves "Does it look right?" "What part doesn't look right?" and "Do I need to change any part?" If there is an error, this kind of reflection makes them realize that they probably do not have the whole word wrong, just one part of it. The students should be encouraged to verbalize to the group or a partner how they used this strategy and how well it worked, thus fostering metacognition.

Writing their understanding in their Spelling Log will further reinforce appreciation and use. This strategy works equally well whether spelling in independent writing or on writing tests. If students are using Word Banks, this strategy becomes more useful. They will be able to recall words as they are written in their book with increasing accuracy, especially if they have marked a clue with a highlighter. Give students many chances to use this strategy in directed practice sessions before expecting them to use it independently. The practice is easily accomplished by saying "We're going to have a quick practice test. I want you to try to use ICE for these words." If the testing situation is not threatening, children enjoy the challenge. The Student Teacher activity (see page 79) also lends itself well to such practice. Have Student Teachers come up and dictate words that they think others will have seen and be able to visualize.

Building Blocks

Building Blocks is a strategy using letter clusters called *morphographs*. Morphographs are groups of letters that convey meaning, such as prefixes and suffixes or Greek and Latin roots. For example, *re* is a sound unit or phoneme that means to repeat or do something over. Instruction focuses on the use of applying structural knowledge to known word parts to build new words. All 70,000 English words cannot be memorized, and this strategy helps expand existing knowledge. Word analysis fosters the awareness that our orthographic system does, indeed, make sense. Spelling *mismanaging* makes sense because it is built from a known word—*manage*—by adding word parts that have meaning. Similarly, *morphographic* makes sense when one considers the Greek origin *morph* (form) and *graphic* (something written). This understanding helps children apply reasoning, not just memory, to spelling.

How to Introduce and Use Building Blocks

Build awareness. Before children can apply morphographic or structural knowledge, they must become aware of it. Awareness and use will grow gradually, most likely beginning with an understanding of plurals and sim-

Why use Building Blocks?	Skill Development
• It develops a mental dictionary. • It encourages word analysis based on meaning. • It strengthens the connection between meaning and spelling. • It emphasizes the predictability of written language. • It facilitates segmentation of longer words into manageable parts. • It facilitates self-monitoring.	• prefixes and suffixes • complex clusters • word origins and derivatives • metacognition • strategy for spelling difficult words • strategy for applying structural knowledge of words

ple endings such as *ing* that occur naturally in speech and are auditorily distinct. Gradually children should come to realize that if they know one word, they really know many. This sounds simplistic, but that is because it is so automatic for us as adults. It is this awareness, or metacognition, that makes Building Blocks a useful spelling strategy. Only with conscious awareness will children be able to use blocks of meaning to build new words.

Opportunities must be structured to ensure observation of morphographs in meaningful text. These opportunities could include cloze activities in which affixes (prefixes and suffixes) have been blanked out are useful to develop awareness. Activities like this may be presented to the whole class or completed in small cooperative groups with attention directed to missing morphographic information. Prompts such as "How did you know to double the t?" and "Why would you only add *d* instead of *ed*?" may be used to promote awareness of the mechanics of using morphographs.

Another way to develop morphographic awareness is to provide structured opportunities to discover the meaning related to the morphographs. For example, create chances for students to see a group of words that have an *er* ending and lead them to discover how the words are similar. This reinforces the predictability of spelling. The Building Blocks method may also be used to facilitate understanding of foreign or ancient word origins. For example, awareness of the root *astro* can be used to build many other words.

Provide direct instruction. When you feel that the students are familiar with the concept of word parts related to meaning, direct instruction may be given in applying their knowledge as a spelling strategy. Tell the students they are going to learn and practice a strategy that that will help them to be able to spell many words when they are writing. Give them the name of the strategy and discuss the analogy of building blocks—many words are built from one known word by adding "blocks" of meaning. Application of Building Blocks is guided by self-questioning. In attempting a new word students should ask themselves the following:

Is there a part of this word I know?

What do I need to change?

Does it look right? (asked after writing)

Usage is modeled first by the teacher and then by peers. The teacher initially demonstrates the thought processes used in spelling a word with a suffix by thinking aloud. (Thinking aloud may take some practice at first. For my first few tries I found it worthwhile to script my lessons ahead of time, but then it got easier.)

Runner. Well I know how to make *run.* That's easy. I know that the *er* ending makes it mean a person that's running. *R-u-n-e-r.* Hmmmm. That doesn't look right. Oh yeah. I need to double the *n* because it's a short vowel.

Present several examples in this manner, selecting words that will not only teach the strategy but will provide a review of the rules of adding affixes. Ask volunteers to share their thinking out loud and let them choose the words they share. Further practice and review using Building Blocks may be facilitated through group activities such as the cloze activity described earlier, personal writing, sharing, group proofreading, and individual writing conferences. A mini-unit is included in Chapter 7 (see pages 105–107) that focuses on adding endings.

Students should record their personal understanding of the orthographic knowledge and application in their Spelling Logs. Prompts could include having them write what they know about word parts and meanings, having them describe how to use the Building Blocks strategy, and having them relate about where or when they think they might use this strategy or why it is useful.

Conclusion

This chapter has described how to teach six generic strategies. The strategies are based on using different methods to spell words, and it is important to teach all six. Students should come to know their own learning strengths and have a choice of strategies that suit their styles and match the word to be spelled. Although taught individually, the strategies are complimentary and it is important to help students be aware that they can often work together. That Reminds Me is a technique that can be used in conjunction with all the others because making connections and drawing on prior knowledge is important. Parts of Looking Good are also applicable to other strategies because visual inspection is to be encouraged. SIP might be the first strategy chosen, but then ICE might be used to spell the syllable. Chapter 6 and Chapter 7 will provide lessons that, in addition to class-writing events, will provide opportunities to practice these strategies in structured activities.

5

Ongoing Assessment and Evaluation of Students' Spelling

I n the past, assessment and evaluation have been done at the end of a unit or project and have signaled completion. In this program, these two processes are seen as an integral, ongoing part of daily activities rather than a separate entity. Traditional spelling programs often place emphasis on marking students' errors on weekly tests and assigning a grade to their spelling ability. This type of evaluation is not always helpful to the student and it does little to help the instructor discover where students are having problems or what lessons he or she should focus on. If we reconceptualize assessment as the vehicle to inform instruction then the goal changes. The focus changes from *testing* to *gathering information* which will provide direction for the next instructional experiences. Such ongoing assessment of all spelling activities that looks at both problems and successes will guide teachers who use the activities in *The Spelling Book*. But how does this kind of assessment work? This chapter will describe techniques that will generate the information necessary for responsive planning and will have application to all the subsequent chapters. In this program, assessment is the ongoing process of gathering information on which to base the following decisions on the next page:

- What phonics do I need to be teaching now?
- Maybe I should teach that unit on endings now?
- Are they ready for Greek word origins?
- Oh no, I haven't taught homonyms yet!

These are questions that can be answered only by gathering information about the individual students within each class, because there are no absolute answers, sequence, or time frame. That is why this method was not designed as prescriptive or presented in a sequence that should be followed, but is assembled as a compilation of activities that could be used to meet many needs and situations. Information upon which to assess the needs and base program decisions is gathered by constantly evaluating lessons and activities as they occur: Did the lesson do what was intended? Are there new directions indicated by the results?

Judgments will reflect a variety of data-gathering methods, including needs noticed in independent writing, in talking to students, and in dictated tests. The needs will vary with every class, depending on students' past experiences and general level of spelling development. The teacher's decisions will reflect current themes and topics being studied, because that is what students will be writing about. Assessment is a valid undertaking only if it is used to plan future learning.

Assessment and Spelling Goals

The logical first step is to revisit the goals of the spelling program and then to identify some of the questions that should be asked to guide assessment. Continual self-questioning, as well as analysis of student responses and actions will provide answers and guidance. In Chapter 3 the goals of this spelling program were identified as:

1. Developing strategies to be used during independent writing.
2. Developing a positive, effortful attitude toward spelling.
3. Developing a good knowledge of sound-symbol relations.
4. Developing a personal understanding of spelling structures.
5. Developing the ability to monitor and self-correct spelling.

All of the activities and strategies in this book have been structured to develop these understandings. Envisioning how to successfully meet these goals in one's class leads to specific questions:

Is the student's spelling improving?

What is the developmental level?

What spelling structures is the student using appropriately?

What phonics knowledge is being used appropriately?

What grammatical structures are being used appropriately?

Is the student able to write technical words?

Does the student consistently write high-frequency words accurately?

Is the student able to spell multisyllable words?

Is the student able to build on known words?

Is the student able to find and fix errors?

Is the student aware of a variety of strategies to use?

Can the student verbalize or explain his or her strategies?

Does the student transfer lesson topics to pragmatic writing?

Are there common error patterns that indicate a need for remediation?

Once we have the questions, it is much easier to find the answers, and the emphasis moves past marks and on to planning.

When assessment is viewed as a planning tool more than a grading tool, it is often necessary to revise and broaden the assessment techniques. The answers to many of the pertinent questions listed earlier would not be evident from a traditional weekly spelling test. Nor would all of the answers be found in a writing sample. A comprehensive, well-rounded assessment includes information from many sources and many writing experiences. The rest of this chapter will present suggestions for gathering student information.

Dictated Tests

Tests of any kind (observational, dictated, or writing analysis) generate information necessary to make good decisions about what to study. Dictated tests may provide some useful information, but one of the challenges with formal measures is the apprehension they generate. In this methodology, the reason for "tests" is gathering information for both student and teacher, not passing a value judgment. It is the information that is important, not the score. Some students (and teachers) need this concept reinforced. Direct teaching and discussion in this area should be included as the program is introduced. Make sure the students share the same idea about assessment as you do.

The value of dictated word tests varies. For example, a student's independent writing may contain few or no errors, but it may be evident that no spelling risks are being taken. New or challenging words are not being used, and independent writing may be overly simplistic. The student may need encouragement to extend his or her use of language and ability to spell. A dictated test would reveal the student's confidence with new or challenging vocabulary. Dictated tests also can focus on specific structural information that has been presented in class. The dictated word lists can be teacher made or selected from several available commercial tests. One of the greatest benefits of the commercial tests is that they present a precompiled word list by orthographic (that is, letter pattern) structure or by word type. It is not generally necessary to dictate the whole test, as it is not the score that is required. It is more useful to select only the words that reflect current teaching.

The questions to be asked in evaluating a dictated commercial test might be: Can the student apply the rule in an isolated situation? Was the student paying attention to the lesson? Does it need to be repeated, perhaps in a different format? Simply marking test questions as right or wrong provides virtually no information on which to base a decision, and no insight into the student's knowledge or thoughts.

Rewrite

Another useful type of dictated test is the rewrite (Buchannan, 1989), a strategy in which a piece of writing completed by the student several weeks or months earlier is dictated, and the student rewrites it without seeing it. The piece of writing may be selected from samples accumulated in writing folders, from earlier entries in logs or notebooks, or from a previous draft. Working with partners, the children decide who will dictate first. One student reads the whole story aloud. It is then repeated sentence by sentence or phrase by phrase, slowly enough for the author to write the words. The original story is not visible to the writer. The finished story is analyzed and compared with the original to determine growth. If desired, or if there is a need for numerical representation, the two pieces of writing can be scored for a percentage of correct words.

This type of test is useful for showing growth over a period of time. Many of the words that had been misspelled previously may now be correct. It also has the advantage of being in the child's own language, which remains contextual. Another interesting effect of this technique is that students generally become self-reflective when presented with their earlier writing saying things such as, "Ooooh! Did I write that? Yuck!" Prompts and questions can be incorporated to facilitate this reflection: "What would you do differently?" Students often are able to articulate the areas of spelling in which they have improved.

Assessing Metacognition

It is not only important to ask oneself questions. If we want to know something about students, we need to ask them. A *metacognitive interview* reveals the child's perceptions, especially in relation to his or her own skills and abilities. As has been stated many times, attitude and self-concept are accurate predictors of success. To gauge attitude we must ask questions.

Writing Conferences: The Teachable Moment

Interviews can take a variety of forms, from a simple 5-minute writing conference between student and teacher to a formal whole-group questionnaire. Questioning techniques are often used as part of the proofreading process, in which the teacher might ask "How did you spell *found*?" "I notice you erased your first try," or "Could you help your friend to spell *found* without just giving the letters?"

Responses will give insights into not only levels of confidence, but strategies being used. A reply of "I made it with a *w* first, but then it didn't look right, so then I thought of *round*, like in that poem, so I changed it to a *u*," would indicate confidence as well as metacognitive awareness of a variety of strategies. However, if the written word was *fonud* (found) and the reply was "I don't know," or "I sounded it out," which is the most common reply if the student does not know what they did, you might want to probe a little further. The comment suggests little spelling conscience or metacognition. It seems more likely that the student either copied the letters backward from a word list, or remembered the word visually (ICE) but mixed up the letters rather than sounding out the word. This student is probably not aware of what he or she did and thus is not able to choose an alternate strategy. A teacher response in this scenario might be as follows:

Teacher: Let me see if I can guess your thinking. It doesn't look like you sounded out that word. I'm guessing that you used ICE. You thought about how the word looks, remembered all the letters, and wrote them down. Am I right?

Student: Yeah. (This type of prompting often validates a strategy that the student is not aware of or may think is the wrong answer.)

Teacher: Did you remember the last part of ICE? To examine or check if the word looks right?

At this point, the student may well locate the reversal independently. If he or she does not, you may direct him or her to a chart or list, or you may write the correct word on a different paper. This is the teachable moment. Have the student visually check the word and make the correction, because having the student rather than the teacher make the correction will reinforce the standard spelling through several modalities—visual (seeing the word), auditory (saying the letters as they are written), and kinesthetic (the arm and hand movements of writing).

The question "Could you help your friend to spell *found*?" provides different information. Consider the student who, although he or she has spelled the word correctly, hesitantly replies "I don't know" or is only able to dictate the correct letters. This snapshot would again suggest a cause for some concern, or at least further inquiry:

Is the child aware of his or her own spelling strategies?

Is he or she able to put them into words?

Is it a lack of confidence in his or her spelling abilities?

Is it shyness?

Is it an isolated incident, because it is a bad day?

If the difficulty lies in awareness of or ability to verbalize strategies, the guess your thinking response described earlier may be appropriate to model language or reinforce useful strategies. Directed questioning or prompting, "Can you tell your friend what is the first thing you do when you use ICE?" may help to break down the task into parts that the student is able to verbalize.

It is important to note that the ability to describe one's thinking or be aware of the learning strategies used may be challenging for students who have not had significant practice in doing this. Our traditional school system has not often supported growth in metacognition, and students may need help. As children are encouraged to think reflectively and understand their own learning, the process gets easier and the benefits are exponential.

Reflections on Thinking and Understanding in Spelling Logs

The Spelling Log is one of the most useful vehicles for assessing understanding of concepts and metacognition. Entries made in response to the following questions or prompts will yield similar information to that in the previous section:

Write about how you spelled the word you are most proud of on today's test.

How would you teach a young person to spell *pirate*?

Write about something that happened or something you heard in your group today that helped you to be a better speller.

Other Spelling Log prompts can be found in Chapter 4.

Perhaps the most productive use of Spelling Logs is to have the students describe what they learned during a particular lesson or activity. This provides not only an invaluable opportunity to reinforce student learning by having them paraphrase or put the information into their own words, but it also provides documented evidence of their level of understanding. It is easy to gauge whether the student has a thorough mastery of the concept presented, whether you have created an awareness of the concept, or whether the lesson has gone completely over the student's head. As noted, competence in all types of reflective thinking or writing is a process that takes time to develop, so do not despair when early responses are brief or simplistic.

Written Interviews or Questionnaires

More comprehensive metacognitive information can be obtained by having students complete a written questionnaire. Although the answers can be scored quantitatively (as will be discussed later), the greatest value lies in the content of the answers. The questions can be structured around any desired focus, but it is important that they invite more than one-word answers. It is often necessary to directly prompt further depth and thought with questions such as, "Do you ever do anything else?" Stating a question in more than one way is also useful. Children may have difficulty explaining their own strategies or thinking, but having them describe how they would help a younger person who was having trouble is in effect the same information. BLM 5, BLM 5A, BLM 6, and BLM 6A show variations of the same theme—questions and sentence starters. Remember, these are examples of questions only and are meant to be adapted for individual classroom use.

Written questionnaires should not be used more than two or three times in a year. Not only do students tire of them, familiarity with the questions makes them suspect there is a "right" answer.

Creating a Scorable Test

To document student growth or when it is important to have a quantitatively scored measure, a questionnaire can be assigned numerical values. The scores obtained will be criterion referenced (compared with expected outcomes for curriculum presented in class) rather than standardized (compared with norms of a wide population). For each question, decide what type of answer you would expect from a highly metacognitive student. Assign that response a value of 2 points. Decide what type of answer would show awareness, but little depth, and assign that answer a value of 1 point. No points would be awarded for incorrect or overly simplistic responses. The total number of points can be converted to a percentage of the maximum number of points possible. When used at the beginning and end of the year, this measure can be useful in evaluating student growth as well as the effectiveness of the metacognitive aspects of the spelling program.

Analysis of Independent Writing

The most powerful source of information on which to base program decisions is analysis of independent writing. It is through this type of assessment that thought processes and levels of awareness become more apparent than any other, because the real goal is to apply spelling knowledge, not to memorize words or be able to talk about spelling.

Writing samples for analysis can come from any source including journals, story drafts (edited or unedited), notetaking activities, reports, projects, or class assignments. All of these writing experiences would provide different information especially if one also took into consideration the context of the activity:

1. Was the student writing a personal experience?
2. Had there been any prewriting activities that would have generated visible word lists or familiarity with the expected vocabulary?
3. Had the piece of writing been proofread by the student, the teacher, a peer, or by a parent?
4. Was the writing done independently or in a group in which a partner would have been available for support?
5. Did the student ask others for assistance or did he or she just sound out the words?

All of these situations are legitimate and valuable and would have a profound affect on the level of spelling competence. In evaluating writing these contextual factors shade the interpretation. For example, if students were writing a summary about a personal experience, the prior knowledge and vocabulary would be significantly different than if they were writing the same summary from events in a book they were reading. It would be important in the analysis to note the context of the writing. Similarly, one would expect substantially higher levels of standard spelling if the students had engaged in prewriting activities such as field experiences, group discussion, or brainstorming because the words would have been seen and heard repeatedly, developing not only a visual memory but a mind-set. Again this affects our judgment of the student. The level of teacher or peer support would also be important information. Our analysis might begin "with the help of a friend __ is able to...." Knowing whether the student attempts new words independently (and what strategy is used), or consistently requests help gives information about attitude and confidence. This may not be quantitative data but it certainly is valuable information.

Checking for Errors and Strengths

Rather than mark up an original piece, it might be preferable to make a photocopy to work on. Go through the copied writing and circle the errors. It is up to you whether to circle errors such as punctuation, capital letters, or names. After the errors are circled, a calculation of percentage of correct spellings may be done. The errors are then recorded in the appropriate space on the Spelling Analysis sheet (BLM 7). For later clarity, it may be useful to record the correct spelling in brackets. The Standard Spellings at the bottom of the sheet is used to record significant words that the student has spelled correctly. These words are important because they document evidence of what the student does know and is applying.

Analysis

Select a piece of writing. The piece need not be lengthy; two to three paragraphs is sufficient. Analyze errors for patterns of error type to learn what spelling processes the student seems to be using. The ability to correctly determine the strategy the student used improves with practice. See boxed copy on this page for things to look for in analyzing writing. Comments may be added that give further information including observations you made while the student was writing or the writing context in which the writing took place. The student samples in Figure 8 on the following pages give a variety of data. Children's spelling errors are not random, and they give guidance for instructional decisions (Tarasoff, 1992; Gentry & Gillet, 1993).

Figure 8 Sample Spelling Error Analysis

If the child wrote	It is likely that the student	It may help to
Mi favrit time was *wan*…	constructed words by sounding them out; used letter names rather than letter sounds (*mi = my*).	teach about word families in which *y* represents the *i* sound; teach about high-frequency words such as *when* and *my*; use word lists to spell longer words.
tow bears *plaed* with…	used a visual approach and reversed letters (*tow = two*). is aware of the *ed* ending.	reinforce visual monitoring.
Jerry and Benji are looking at the jeep *becus ther* are dogs in it.	used visual memory to spell *becus* and *ther*.	prompt the child to inspect the word when it is written.
went to the police *stashon*	used phonics to sound out *shon*.	teach complex letter clusters such as *tion*.
He was a war *hearo*	used the known word *hear* to construct *hero*.	praise the attempt to build on the known word; write the word two or three times and have the student select the best one based on visual cues.
the *anumls weat* to the *rvr* to drink…	used phonics because the beginning and ending sounds are appropriate; is able to hear medial sounds; omitted the *n* sound in *went*; used a visual strategy for *went* (*a* is similar to *n*) and perhaps knew there should be a letter there; is able to segment multisyllable words.	build on cluster families such as *ent*. reinforce high-frequency words.
wet (went) to *cap* (camp) and …jump off the *dok* (dock)	omitted the prenasal consonants (*n* in *went* and *m* in *camp*) but not in *jump*; may have used a visual strategy to spell *jump*.	teach cluster families for words with prenasal consonants.
Onec upon a time…a *gint stolle* a bag of gold	probably used a visual strategy for *once* and *stole* because approximations are close and the other words are correct; knew the double *ll* pattern; used phonics for *giant*.	encourage visual monitoring; review words with double consonant patterns.
The girl was *skaired* she would lose her *daller* (dollar) before she got to the *stour* (store).	aware of letter cluster patterns (*air, our*); uses rhyming patterns to spell new words (*your* for *store*, *ball* for *dollar*).	review cluster patterns for multiple ways to represent the same sound.
One day there *waz* a little terrier *naemd* Terry.	spelled *named* with visual strategies; tried to sound out *was*.	encourage this student to visually monitor words; focus on high-frequency words.
She *sriemd* (screamed) and *jumpt* away.	is overreliant on phonics to spell new words; made no attempt to use suffix rules.	encourage use of strategies other than phonics; teach endings rules.

(continued)

Figure 8 Sample Spelling Error Analysis (continued)

If the child wrote	It is likely that the student	It may help to
She *tok* (took) *los* (lots) of the nuts because she *waz hagree* (hungry)…	may have a problem with phonemic awareness; missed individual sounds in *screamed*, *lots*, and distorted sounds in *hungry*.	assess and provide training in phonemic awareness.
He *spoted* him playing marbles in the Grand Challenge. He *yelld* Good luck	has good knowledge of complex clusters (*challenge*, *marbles*); took no notice of suffix rules or quotation marks.	provide instruction in adding endings and use of quotation marks.
Tthe next day I went *bake* to the *tomstone* at the *gravyard*. It *siad* Billy *mcgee*. I *pikt* up my *sweter* and	probably overgeneralized the final *e* rule; probably sounded out *tombstone* and *graveyard* but missed the silent letters; is overreliant on phonics (*sweater*, *pikt*); may be weak in applying correct capital letters.	assess capital letter knowledge; use word families to reinforce words such as *back*, *pick*, and *bake* as well as word families with silent letters; teach segmentation of compound words. focus on strategies other than sound it out, including Building Blocks to teach endings.

Recording Information

Information about student learning is gathered from a wide variety of sources and contexts. Assessment is sometimes planned, sometimes casual, and sometimes unexpected. The purpose of assessment is to produce data to inform program planning and to report to parents, but the details generated can be overwhelming or unused if they are not documented and organized. The myriad information gathered must be compiled in a functional format if it is to be useful in guiding instructional decisions. Periodically completing a student spelling profile using a Spelling Behaviors Checklist such as BLM 8 helps to organize information and focus thinking. It provides a useful focal point for discussing student progress with parents, assisting you in helping them to understand the goals of the spelling program as well as their child's current learning. Both the Class Spelling Profile (BLM 2) and the Expected Learning Outcomes List (BLM 1) are also organizational formats that assist in keeping track of student progress and planning instruction.

6

Getting Started With Spelling Instruction

There is no optimum time to begin using the spelling methodologies described here. They represent a philosophy about helping children become more fluent in their written expression. Implementation can begin at any time during the year. Other than directly teaching the generic spelling strategies described in Chapter 4, there is no sequential beginning or end. However, it is important that students share the mindset, so it is crucial to set the stage for learning at the outset of adopting the philosophy. Doing so creates motivation and the mindset necessary to learn.

The introductory strategies and lessons presented here should reinforce the message of spelling as an exploration of language occurring in a risk-free environment in which the student's individual thinking is valued. The activities included in this chapter introduce the routines and procedures used throughout the school year. Each overview gives a summary of the introductory strategy or routine, highlights the goals and rationale, and provides procedural steps for implementing it.

Setting the Stage

Preparing for the year with an open, honest discussion about the usefulness of learning to spell is important. Students will retain learning and it will be more real and more important if students are learning in order to meet their own needs, rather than simply to meet the curriculum. Share your ideas and have students share their ideas about when, why, and for whom spelling is an important thing to learn. Ask them what they think makes a good spelling program. It is important to remember that there are no wrong answers, ideas, or opinions.

Why use Setting the Stage?	Skill Development
• It helps students understand and take ownership for the real goals of learning to spell. • It sets the teacher's expectations. • It begins the process of creating a risk-free environment. • It hooks students because it acknowledges when, where, and why spelling is important. • It indicates that spelling is not just something laid down by the teacher.	• positive, effortful attitude • metacognition

How to Use Setting the Stage

The following discussion questions can be used as a guide in introducing spelling instruction:

- Is spelling important? What makes you think that?
- Is it always important? (Compare, for instance, a job application and a grocery list.)
- What should the goals of a spelling program be?
- Which is more important—tests or independent writing?
- How should spelling be marked or evaluated?
- Who is the best speller you know? How does he or she spell words?

Model and encourage students to be sincere in their responses. For example, when I ask if spelling is always important, many children respond "Yes, of course." (They probably say this because they predict it to be the answer I want to hear!) I usually respond by telling them the story of the time my mother chastised me and corrected the word *broccoli* on my grocery list. Is it really important that my grocery be proofread? Or does it really matter if there are a few mistakes in the directions I jot down to get somewhere? What if I am writing a letter to a friend? Or applying for a job? It is important to be realistic about the importance of this skill and to let students know when it is less vital to spell correctly. Some students honestly think the most important thing about learning to spell is getting a good mark on the test because this is what they have learned from parents and teachers. Only through open discussion can we change this perception.

Encouraging input from students about the goals and evaluation of the spelling program, about the best ways to spell new words, about when spelling lessons should occur, and about which pieces of writing should be error-free models teach students that their opinions are valued and respected and that it is acceptable, even desirable, to express diverse opinions. Sincere respect for diversity is a powerful factor in creating an environment in which students are comfortable taking the risks necessary to become good spellers.

Think of a Time 1–2–3

Think of a Time (adapted from Brownlie, Close, Wingren, *Tomorrow's Classroom Today: Strategies for Creating Active Readers, Writers and Thinkers*, 1990) is a great ice breaker. It encourages students to focus on positive feelings and successes related to spelling and, at the same time, helps them to understand that other people make mistakes too. This activity shows children that there are many different ways to spell and, if one strategy does not work, they have to try a different one. Children are amazed (as are most adults I have done this activity with) when they see all the various spelling strategies listed on the board or on chart paper.

Think of a Time provides a forum to establish class goals. Students should understand that it is more important to learn to use a few spelling strategies that work for a multitude of words than to attempt to memorize all 70,000 words in our language. Participants are encouraged to view a concept from three different viewpoints: as an actor, as a witness, and as a cause of the action. Students are grouped in triads and, through three focus questions, reflect on the focus concept and share their ideas.

Why use Think of a Time 1–2–3?	Skill Development
• It promotes a positive self-concept and feelings of success.	• positive attitude and confidence
• It encourages participants to share and verbalize personal strategies for success, as well as become aware of other people's strategies.	• strategy awareness
• It facilitates the realization that nobody is perfect and that everybody has faced difficulties that can be overcome.	• metacognition

Introducing Think of a Time 1–2–3

Divide the class into groups of three and have them assign each member a number from 1 to 3. Direct the groups to, "Think of a time when you were successful at spelling a really hard word." After a few seconds of thinking time, have each person share his or her experience or strategies within his or her group. After the small-group exchange, have volunteers share their experience and strategies with the large group.

Next direct all number 1s to relocate to another group. Ask the group to "Think of a time when someone else helped you to spell a really hard word." Have them share within their group once again. Encourage volunteers to share with the whole class.

Direct all number 2s to relocate to a new group. This time have the groups "Think of a time when you helped someone else spell a really hard word" and share this with their group. This time the strategies that are shared should be recorded on a chart and posted. Draw attention to the number and variety of ways that people go about spelling new or difficult words.

After the small- and large-group sharing, have the participants return to their original triads. Have the participants reflect on the process and the concept in their triads and then personally in their Spelling Logs.

Gathering Initial Data

It is always useful for both you and the student to establish a baseline from which to start. It is necessary, however, for students to understand that this assessment is for information gathering only and will not go on their report card. Students are more likely to be self-evaluative if they see monitoring as purposeful rather than threatening.

Initial data can be gathered in a number of ways that can be decided on by the teacher and the students. It is useful to have more than one kind of measure, however. Chapter 5 includes a complete discussion of assessment and evaluation.

Independent Writing Sample

An independent writing sample will reflect the student's everyday use of spelling. The writing sample can be obtained from any independent writing the student has done including journals (edited or unedited) and story drafts. Content writing is acceptable as long as it reflects the child's natural language and spelling. If desired, the sample can be calculated to show the percentage of correct spelling by dividing the number of words by the number of errors.

Standardized Tests

A standardized spelling test will also provide valuable information. Besides a score (which should always be taken with a grain of salt), it reveals patterns and misconceptions, such as problems with phonetics, irregular words, or homonyms. Some students may show a very high level of accuracy in their independent writing, but a standardized test may show that they are, in fact, using only relatively simple words in their writing and will find more complicated words challenging. Encouragement and support may be needed to extend these students' vocabulary and spelling skills.

A misspelling analysis of the test, as described in Figure 8 on pages 65–66, should be completed by the teacher. This reveals the types of errors made by the student. The analysis information, when shared with the student, can form personal and class spelling goals.

Spelling Interview or Questionnaire

A spelling interview or questionnaire (BLM 5 or BLM 6), provides valuable and often surprising information about a student's use of spelling strategies. It may reveal the level of metacognitive thinking and direction. This knowledge is key for program planning. Questionnaires can be administered to the whole class in a group session or to individual students orally.

Generic Spelling Strategies

Generic spelling strategies are described in Chapter 4. They are applicable to spelling in *any* context. They define the steps that good spellers use to spell new words in a variety of situations. Each of the six strategies should be introduced early in the program to ensure that students use them during all writing and during word-study activities. Direct instruction in strategic spelling is the basis for teaching children how to spell instead how to memorize.

Why teach generic strategies?	Skill Development
• They emphasize spelling instead of memorizing. • They give children a plan of attack for new words. • They develop metacognition. • They support application of new word knowledge. • They encourage a positive attitude.	• strategy development • metacognition • positive attitude

Introducing Generic Spelling Strategies

All the spelling strategies described in Chapter 4 should eventually be taught to students to support and complement any other spelling instruction they receive. The strategies should be introduced gradually, but early in their program. It is helpful to have engaged in the type of discussion described earlier in the Setting the Stage and Think of a Time sections to introduce the concept of strategic spelling. Always introduce a new strategy by telling the students that the strategy can help them spell new words when they are writing. Give the strategy a name so it is easier for student to remember.

Encourage discussion about when, where, and how this strategy could be used, providing examples of specific words and contexts. Have students paraphrase the strategy in their Spelling Logs and reflect on how they will use the strategy in their writing. Suggestions for introducing each of the strategies are given in Chapter 4.

Give students many opportunities to practice and internalize each new strategy before introducing another. After they have had some practice with each strategy, review the steps with them.

Word Lists

Research into spelling has resulted in a variety of word lists. There are lists that show words to be taught at different grade levels, words for diagnostic spelling tests, words that cause common errors, words for various areas of word study, and frequently written words. Students often find it interesting that adult experts spend a great deal of time studying children's writing and are intrigued to hear these results. A good introduction to spelling instruction might be to have students try to guess the most common error at their grade level or the top 10 most frequently written words. One source for these lists is *Teaching Spelling: Canadian Word Lists and Instructional Techniques* by Ves Thomas (1979). Discussion about the research and the words lists not only generates interest in spelling, but helps to create the mind set and reinforces the attitude that spelling is important.

Most Frequently Written Words

Most Frequently Written Words have been of particular value to spelling instruction. Facilitating a discussion about what words children write most often leads to their acknowledgment that some words are important to know without having to think about their spelling. Although it is useful to accept the published list of frequently used words, I have found it both fun and worthwhile to have the class determine its own list. The lists were determined for a different time and a different place and language changes.

Why create a Frequent-Word List?	Skill Development
• It motivates students to learn a core spelling vocabulary. • It focuses on a specified list of words that are necessary for writing fluency. • It promotes a positive attitude. • The list is displayed in the classroom and provides a quick, visual reference for use in writing.	• metacognition • frequently used words

Introducing Most Frequently Written Words

Following the discussion described above, have the class brainstorm for the top 100 words they believe they use most often (you may want to find fewer depending on the age of the class). Resist the temptation to give them the words. If words are suggested that are not high-frequency words, encourage the class to decide whether to include them or not.

The words should be listed on the board or chart paper, and later put on a chart for permanent display in the room. After the brainstorming, the words should be sorted into alphabetical order (this can be done as a cooperative group activity or by the teacher), and a copy should be provided for each student. Depending on the class and the time available, the words can be typed for the students or they can copy the words. They should be copied in list form for easy scanning. It is best to separate the letter groups of words (that is, all the *a*'s in one group, all the *b*s in another).

Most Frequently Written Words can be kept in your students' personal Word Banks to be used for reference and for use in spelling tests. They should be copied or cut and sorted onto the correct page according to their initial letter. I have found it useful to give the class a spelling test on these words after they have entered them into their books. Again, this reinforces the efficacy of learning these words. The test may be repeated periodically throughout the year to monitor success.

Establishing Routines

It is important to establish some routine procedures early in the program. The spelling tools that were described earlier in the book will be used throughout the year, and it is worthwhile spending time in establishing routines and expectations early. This will facilitate success for students and save headaches for the teacher. Frequently written words are discussed earlier in this chapter; an overview of the other three tools follows. For a more thorough discussion of how to introduce these tools, see Chapter 3.

Spelling Logs

Because personal observation, reflection, and metacognitive development are the prime goals of this spelling method, the Spelling Log is an essential component and should be introduced from the onset. Setup and use of spelling logs is described on pages 35–36. Establish the types of responses you expect to find when you read the books. Explain to students that although there may not be a right answer, you expect thought and effort to be evident in the entries. The students should know that their notes will help you to see what they understand and what you need to teach or reteach. It is essential, however, that students understand their Spelling Logs will not be marked.

Word Banks

Word Banks are personal dictionaries that are used for reference during independent writing and that provide the words for personal spelling tests. An overview of how to introduce Word Banks is provided on pages 36–38. Establish rules for use of Word Banks early: words should be important to the student, they should be in list form, they should be printed neatly, and above all they must be spelled correctly.

Spelling "Tests"

Both research and children in classes I have taught have convinced me that spelling tests can be beneficial in learning to spell. The "tests" described in Chapter 3 do not, however, refer to traditional tests where predetermined word lists are studied and memorized and the test is administered and marked by the teacher. The procedure for introducing "tests" can be found on pages 38–39.

Generic Lessons

The lessons described in the rest of this chapter are generic in nature. They are specific teaching techniques that may be used with any content, in any context in which the goal is facilitation of critical thinking, a focus on process rather than product, and interactive learning. They differ from the lessons described in Chapter 7 in that they are not specifically designed to direct word study, although they lend themselves well to that focus. Because they are non-specific frameworks they may be used over and over to teach or review almost any concept. For example, Mental Modeling is a process that will be used consistently to introduce new concepts because it is an excellent way to give students insights into the thinking process behind spelling. Student Teacher is a reciprocal teaching strategy that works well for giving review in using SIP but is equally effective in practicing high-frequency words. Daily Find and Fix and Proofreading are whole-group structures that use children's writing as the basis for instruction and practice. Again they may be used to meet a variety of goals and with a variety of topics or genre. It is not suggested that all the techniques described here be introduced or taught in any kind of order. In fact, you may not choose to use any of them. They are simply helpful vehicles for teaching spelling.

Mental Modeling

Mental Modeling is a way of showing children how to do something they don't yet know how to do by providing a model for them to follow. The focus is on attempting to describe or make visible for children the thinking processes used by expert spellers, not just the procedural steps. It is a strategy that involves attempting to think aloud as a new word is being spelled. Mental Modeling may be done by both teachers and students.

Introducing Mental Modeling.

Present the modeling in the context of meaningful writing, not in an artificial context such as a workbook page. As words are needed, describe the

Why use Mental Modeling?	Skill Development
• It encourages children to view spelling in a thoughtful, problem-solving manner. • It makes the strategies of expert spellers more obvious. • It provides explicit information about the spelling process, which minimizes the guesswork. • It encourages the student to consciously direct the reasoning process. • It shows, by example, that expert spellers monitor their spelling and make adaptations as they write.	• metacognition • all areas

thoughts and reasoning that might be connected to spelling them. Modeling should include using semantic (meaning) clues, syntactic (language) clues, and phonics (sound-symbol) clues as well as self-questioning.

> *Satisfaction*—that's a big word! I'll say it in parts. That will make it easier. *Sat*, that's easy. *Iz* sounds like *i-z*, but I know it's *i-s*. *Fak*. Hmm I wonder if it's *c* or *k*? Usually it's *c* I'll try that. *Shun* I know that's *t-i-o-n*.

> *Piece*—This is one of those words where there are two words that sound the same. Which one is it? *Piece* of paper. Oh yeah, Josh drew that piece of pie to help him remember it is spelled like *pie*. It must be *p-i-e-c-e*.

> *Careful*—I'll make *care* first and add the ending. *C-a-r-e-f-u-l*—does it have one *l* or two? I can never remember. I'll try both ways and see which one looks right.

> *Pirate*—Oh, I saw that word on that book I was looking at. Let's see if I can get a picture of the letters.

Statements like these model the thinking strategies used in spelling and make them acceptable and valuable.

Model flexibility. Change strategies if one method doesn't work:

> *Trouble*—I'll use SIP. *Tru-bel, t-r-u-b-e-l*. I'm sure that's wrong! I think the cluster is *l-e* at the end, but I'm not sure of the rest. Maybe I have it in my Word Bank.

Provide opportunities for students to discuss and share their reasoning strategies to encourage conscious choices.

Proofreading

Almost everything that is written is proofread to some degree, whether it is a quick glance over a word or paragraph or a formal word-by-word analysis. The ability to proofread one's own writing is integral to the spelling process, but it is not necessarily a skill that all children will acquire naturally. It is, however, a process that can be nurtured and guided. Successful proofreading requires two distinct steps, both of which can cause difficulties. Writers must first be able to locate the errors within their work, and they then must be able to access strategies to correct them. Orthographic knowledge is obviously vital to success in this area, but equally important is the student's attitude. It must be confident and thoughtful, reflecting the perception that "there is something I can do to get the right spelling."

Why Is Proofreading So Important?

Proofreading activities provide an incredible opportunity for both teaching and learning. By focusing on personal errors in a supportive manner the child is able to see, hear about, experience, and rethink a misconception. This happens not when the child's work is proofread and the right answers provided are by a teacher or peer but when the child is involved in the process. Learning occurs when the child looks at and analyzes personal writing, becoming aware of the standard form and of making links to his or her existing knowledge structure. Teachers and peers can facilitate the process by helping to locate errors and by sharing their thinking and strategies for spelling the

Mental Modeling is introduced effectively during whole-group instruction, using other lessons like Cloze Passages or Find and Fix on the overhead. Notetaking demonstrations may also provide practical modeling time. As students become familiar with the process, it is important to gradually relinquish control to them. Opportunities to hear a variety of experts share their strategies reinforces risk taking and confidence. In addition, if a student does not understand or feel comfortable with one spelling method, he or she may respond to another.

word. Hearing how others think enables the child to clarify misconceptions and hear spelling strategies discussed in a meaningful context. Being involved in the process ensures that the child feels in control and becomes aware that spelling is not a magical process known only to others.

How To Teach Proofreading

Continuous practice. Proofreading is not a one-shot lesson, but a process that continues to develop and mature with ability to spell. Continual practice will reinforce new learning and build a necessary, lifelong writing habit. There is no single format for proofreading that applies to all situations, so children must have experience in proofreading in many contexts and with many types of words and writing.

Mechanics versus semantics. It is not an easy task to separate spelling from the context in which it is written. The mind automatically jumps ahead and predicts (or remembers) what comes next. Even excellent spellers may not see mistakes, especially in their own work, because they read rather than analyze the words. Professional proofreaders combat this problem by reading material backwards. Students like to act like professionals and enjoy this strategy. It forces them to focus on what the word looks like. An alternative strategy is to point to the words as they go through or use a ruler to guide the eyes more effectively.

Self-monitoring. Proofreading should not be limited to stories or lengthy writing. Self-monitoring should be automatically built into any spelling strategy used. Students should be encouraged to check their spelling of any word that was new to them. "Does it look, sound, and feel right?" Again, this is a skill that often requires direct instruction.

Author's mumble. This is a strategy in which students read a piece of writing in a very quiet (but not silent) voice. Only they should be able to hear themselves. This encourages them to focus on the words that are actually on the page, rather than what they thought they had written. More importantly, it allows them to hear the sound of the language as well as see the words.

Initially, students need to be encouraged to reread their work to check to see if it sounds right and looks right. "Were there any letters, words, or ideas left out or substituted?" "Did it say what you intended?" "Make sure you read the words as they are written!" As students become comfortable with the fact that everyone makes errors as they write the first draft, they often come to view the process as a game, and become able to laugh at the silly mistakes they find. This attitude that making mistakes is acceptable as long as we fix them is one we want to develop. Author's Mumble should be encouraged with all writing before it is to be read by any audience. Even though it is not acceptable to mark spelling in journals or learning logs, it is a good idea to have students do an Author's Mumble to self-check for glaring errors and legibility.

Daily Find and Fix

Using pieces of writing from volunteers, frequent or daily whole-class find and fix activities model and provide instruction and practice in proof-

Why use Daily Find and Fix?	Skill Development
• It models, not only the process of finding spelling errors, but the application of strategies to make corrections.	• proofreading
	• metacognition
• It provides an opportunity to teach spelling or word knowledge in context. This instruction will come from both the students and the teacher.	• all areas of skills and knowledge
• It provides an opportunity for shared thinking and Mental Modeling by both teacher and classmates.	
• It builds metacognitive awareness because children verbalize their understanding and strategies.	

reading, as well as opportunities for instruction. Writing samples are put on the overhead and proofread by classmates. The samples used can be selected to focus on specific structures or patterns. Suggestions from the group should include both the necessary change and rationale.

Introducing Find and Fix

Promote discussion about the benefits and necessity of being able to proofread and the fact that we can learn from one another. Ask for volunteers to share a piece of writing to be proofread. (Telling students that you need writing that has some errors makes even the poor spellers more confident in participating.) If the lettering on the writing sample is not dark enough to photocopy, it may have to be darkened with a pen; students are usually willing to do this. If the writing sample is long, it is not necessary to complete the whole story. Five to ten minutes is sufficient time for this lesson.

A particular portion of the story may have errors that would provide useful information for the group (for example, errors in specific phonics structures, punctuation, or grammar). Make sure this part of the story is proofread, even if other parts are left out. Using the suggestions from the previous section, model the proofreading process. Go through the whole selection first to get a sense of the story. Then go through more slowly, inspecting each word. Have students raise their hand if they think a word should be checked. This deemphasizes the idea of right and wrong, especially because all writers will find things that they might want to check. When a suggestion for change is given, it should be accompanied by the reason for the suggestion. When the session is complete, the author is given the correction to use—the reward for brave sharing!

Student Teacher

Student Teacher is a lesson adapted from The Reciprocal Teaching described in *Creating Independence Through Student-Owned Strategies* (Santa, 1996), in

<table>
<tr><td>

Why use Student Teacher?
- It provides opportunities for practice in applying skills and strategies, e.g., SIP.
- It encourages verbalization (metacognitive awareness) of spelling strategies.
- It promotes interactive learning.
- It provides opportunity for monitoring student progress.

</td><td>

Skill Development
- all areas of knowledge and skills

</td></tr>
</table>

which children get to play teacher. This encourages internalization of skills and strategies. And what better way to play than with a real class? With gradually increasing independence, volunteers teach their classmates a concept or lead a discussion. The outline here gives practice in using the SIP strategy, but students become adept at facilitating the discussion on many topics.

Introducing Student Teacher*

Tell the children they are going to have a spelling test in which they will practice the SIP strategy. Dictate a few multisyllable words and have volunteers share how they sounded the words in parts and spelled them.

Prepare cards with multisyllable words printed in black and suggested word parts (syllables) marked in red. Tell the children that they are going to start doing some of the teaching, because they are such experts. At this point, a discussion about teaching as a way to help learn and remember things is a good way to promote metacognition.

Hand out the cards, face down. These are the teacher's guide or answer key (this makes the activity less threatening for many children). Hand out cards to everyone, even though not all students will have, or want, a chance to teach that day. This emphasizes that all students are expected to participate and gives all students a chance to see a word broken into parts. It is likely to provide a visual record that the student will be able to recall later.

Have the students read their word to themselves. (Help individuals as necessary.) Ask a volunteer to come to the front and be the teacher by saying, "Mr. or Ms. *Name* is the teacher." Children love being called Mr. or Ms. The student can use the prepared cards to follow your example of giving a spelling test and calling on classmates to share answers. The Student Teacher can dictate two or three words, then give another Student Teacher a chance. Initially the adult teacher will need to guide and prompt the questioning process, but the support needed from the adult will decrease gradually. Students love to imitate teacher behaviors such as getting attention and praising good answers, and this should be encouraged.

The role of the teacher at this point is to model the language in a variety of ways:
Dictate the word and use it in a sentence.
Have the class use SIP to write the word in their Spelling Logs.
Have volunteers share how they sounded the word and how they spelled it.
Write the suggested answers on the board, either separating the clusters or drawing a slash between them.
Draw attention to common clusters.
Legitimize sounding words different ways.

* From *Creating Independence Through Student-Owned Strategies*, 2nd edition, edited by Carol Santa. Copyright © 1996 by Kendall/Hunt Publishing Company. Used with permission.

Extended Application

Do not limit the use of this lesson to SIP. Encourage students to practice other strategies too. The practice test used to initiate this lesson can focus on the use of any or all of the spelling strategies, as long as the adult has prepared cards or a list that can be used as a guide. The teacher's guide promotes confidence and ensures that all students can participate, regardless of spelling ability.

Student Teachers can provide quick drill and practice with brainstormed or thematic words by dictating words from the list and calling on others to share their answers and strategies used. (This is also a good way to fill a few extra minutes.) The adult may plan a Student Teacher activity to focus on a desired or needed spelling structure such as multisyllable words, homonyms, or prefixes and suffixes.

The process of Student Teacher is appropriate for many diverse learning situations, not just a spelling dictation. I have used it with math practice, cloze passages, and answers to written questions.

Cloze Encounters

This is a cloze lesson in which groups of letters are blanked out of the text, and the correct spelling is filled in by the whole class or individual student. The words, letters, or clusters are selected by the teacher to highlight desired word structures. It is best done in a group or supported situation in which children are encouraged to verbalize and explain their thinking.

Introducing Cloze Passages

Choose a piece of text that relates to themes or units currently being studied. The text should be a complete literary unit: It could be a letter, message, short story, poem, or informational material. Words or parts of words are blanked out or covered up. If necessary, the writing may be enlarged on a photocopier to create sufficient room to write.

Why use cloze passages?	Skill Development
• They provide opportunities to plan lessons that ensure students observe word structures. • They encourage children to activate their own thoughts and verbalize their spelling strategies. • They help children gain insight into the spelling process because students observe spelling structures in context and hear generalizations or rules put into words. • They are an effective means of teaching skills such as phonics and structural analysis within a meaningful text. • They promote risk-taking.	• all skill and knowledge areas • metacognition

Letters or clusters may be left in or blanked out to focus on specific phonics rules or generalizations. The text may be presented on an overhead projection or chart paper and read together. Individuals are called on to supply the missing words or letters and give reasons to support their choices. The activity may be started as a group and completed independently, however, it is always most beneficial to encourage students to discuss their suggestions by working with partners.

As a group or partner activity, children are encouraged to think aloud as they fill in the blanks. There often is not one right answer. Any word is acceptable as long as it sounds right, makes sense, and fits with the letters that have been left in. Observations and generalizations should be shared at the end of the activity and understandings recorded in Spelling Logs. The Logs provide a record of learning for teacher assessment.

This activity also provides a worthwhile homework activity for students. Parents are able to help their child, and gain awareness of how well he or she is able to apply spelling knowledge. They should be encouraged to share their spelling strategies with their child.

Sort and Classify

Sort and Classify is a cooperative language strategy in which words or ideas are recorded, cut into separate units, and then sorted into categories. Encouraging student-generated categories provides practice in critical thinking, but teacher-directed sorting may be used for specific purposes. Sort and Classify has a wide variety of applications in every context from spelling to math.

Introducing Sort and Classify

This activity is introduced using words and ideas than have been brainstormed or selected for use from current study. These are recorded on paper (you can use BLM 9), sentence strips, or cards. Heterogeneous cooperative groups of three or four students are formed and one copy of the words and ideas is given to each group. The groups are instructed to cut up the words and sort them into categories. The words may be grouped by semantics (meaning), or word patterns (auditory or visual). Most often students should be encouraged to determine their own categories with minimal teacher direction, although direction may be given for specific purposes, such as, "Sort the words into categories according to the sounds you hear." Instructing students to sort words a second way after they have completed one way helps to extend thinking beyond the obvious.

Extended Application

Sorting and classifying can be used in a wide variety of contexts:

- sorting brainstormed words into categories according to sounds, letter clusters, endings, or parts of speech;

Why use Sort and Classify?	Skill Development
• It teaches students to cut words or ideas into individual parts, which allows student to physically manipulate language • It uses familiar language thus allowing children to focus on the skill or concept being taught. • It breaks down language and information into manageable parts. Students are more able to read the parts and learn the concepts. • Manipulating words encourages students to acquire a visual memory for the words thus facilitating sight vocabulary development. • The supportive cooperative group invites participation from all students, allowing them to work with content ideas and language even if independent reading or writing is challenging. • Classifying new knowledge and creating links to prior knowledge helps students to understand, retain, and retrieve information. • Encouraging students to classify and reclassify information facilities extended thinking skills.	• metacognition • visual analysis of words • all areas of word knowledge

- sorting brainstormed ideas (prior knowledge) into categories or subtopics for research;
- sorting words or ideas to match pictures;
- sorting quotes from a story or article according to appropriate character or incident;
- sorting brainstormed prior knowledge about a new topic into things students are *sure of* and things students *think may be true*; and
- sorting words according to feelings generated or senses evoked.

7

Guided Word-Study Lessons

C hildren need three things to become competent spellers—a positive, thoughtful *attitude*; *word knowledge*; and *specific strategies* to apply their knowledge. Ways to encourage a positive, thoughtful attitude were discussed in Chapters 3 and 6 and generic spelling strategies were presented in Chapter 4. This chapter will deal with how we can help students increase their knowledge about our language.

In traditional spelling lessons a rule or concept is taught, and children are expected to "learn" or memorize the rule as presented. However, as noted in Chapter 2, research has confirmed that having children develop personal interpretations about how language works is more effective than having them simply memorize words. But it is not realistic to believe that all children will develop all the knowledge they need by immersing them in reading and writing. It is our job as teachers to orchestrate the learning. The activities included in this chapter differ from traditional lessons in that they are not exercises with a specific right answer. They are carefully planned *guided word studies* that attempt to structure opportunities for children to explore words and language in ways that will ensure they develop their own generalizations. The lesson formats are similar to the generic lessons described in Chapter 6, but specific language goals are identified and addressed for each activity. The investigations are integrated into the total curriculum currently being studied, building on words that are part of the present classroom conversation.

The lesson plans are grouped as areas of study (see Figure 9). Although it is not necessary to use these lessons in the order given, they have been presented in order of spelling development. All children will benefit from working with Frequently Used Words. The Orthography section focuses on the art or *how to* of spelling including the art of strategy use, how to use mnemonic clues for difficult words, and how to use adjectives or structural parts. Cluster activities develop knowledge about common groups of letters and their associated sounds. The lessons on Word Origins require the most sophisticated thinking.

These lessons are meant to be starting points only. The needs, interests, and context of each individual class will dictate the pace. Most of these lessons are variations on the teaching strategies described in Chapter 4 and may be used repeatedly with different words or spelling patterns. For example, several of them are cloze passages that will be used over and over by simply using a different passages that focuses attention on a different language concept.

Figure 9 Specific Spelling Lessons

Frequently Used Words	Orthography	Clusters
Demon Cards	Guess My Thinking	Cluster Collection
Cloze Encounters	Write A Picture	Letter Clusters
Frequent-Word Sort		

Error Analysis	Homonyms	Word Origins
Data Collection	Homonym Cloze	What's in a Name?
Marking Guide	Semantic Lists	Making Meaning
Writer's Report Card	Homonym Link-Ups	Word Wheels
	Mnemonics	Word Origin Cloze
	Homonym Books	
	Hilarious Homonyms	

Five-Minute Lessons

ABC Order Cards	Cluster Relay	Check it Out
List Cloze	Letter Ladder	Find Some
Make Words	Make a Rule	

Adding Endings: A Mini-Unit

Cloze passage
Flower Power
Group Proofing

Frequently Used Words—Words Worth Remembering

As I stressed in Chapters 3 and 6, the words students identify as ones that they use often when writing are worth remembering. In creating a Most Frequently Written Words list (see page 74), students will have developed some ownership for and personal motivation to learn the correct spelling for these words, although some students may require prompting to use the standard spelling. It is therefore useful to structure lessons and activities to assist them.

Successfully spelling frequently used words during writing requires the use of a variety of strategies that go beyond memorization. Students should be encouraged to apply all the spelling strategies they have been taught for recalling the correct spelling. In addition, planning some specific activities that draw attention to visual structures of the words or to the sound of the words will give students a greater chance of success.

Motivation is a key ingredient in dealing with high-frequency words. In our attempts to encourage students to use invented spelling to express their ideas, a few have mistakenly come to the conclusion that spelling never counts, and continue to spell a word a different way each time it comes up in the story they are writing. Gentle guidance may be needed to give the student the confidence to continue to write and to begin to take responsibility for spelling some words correctly. Modeling and personal writing conferences help the children to acknowledge their own spelling demons and discuss strategies.

The suggestions listed in this section are some ways in which students may gain competence in developing and using a core spelling vocabulary.

Demon Cards

Demon Cards are file cards on which students make a list of the correct spelling of their personal "demon" words. The card is kept on their desk, in their binder, in their writing folder—wherever it will be the most accessible for each student. The card is used as a quick reference during writing. Demon Cards may not be necessary or desirable for all students. These scaffolds are useful for students who have the most difficulty with spelling, especially when it comes to high-frequency words. The easier it is to quickly locate the correct spelling, the more likely the student is to make the effort to do so. Using Demon Cards saves time in looking up the word on a list, in Word Banks, or in dictionaries. Students who consistently spell such words correctly would not need this type of support.

Introducing and using Demon Cards. Demon Cards may be introduced to the whole class or to individual students as required. Hold a discussion acknowledging the importance of expressing ideas.

Tell students that some words are a problem and that you are going to provide a strategy to help. Acknowledge that having to stop and look up words that are used many times during the story interferes with creating the story. Tell students you know how much easier it would be if those words were immediately available. Have students choose a maximum of 10–20

Even though there may be lists of such words posted in the room, looking for the list and then searching through it for the needed word may be too cumbersome for many students. The goal here is to make it easy for the student to be successful. Repeated use of the correct spelling, in meaningful context, will eventually create fluency.

Why use Demon Cards?	Skill Development
• They provide a quick reference system that is easy for challenged spellers to use. • They reinforce the idea that some attempt should be made to spell high-frequency words correctly. • They make a personalized list containing only the words which each student needs.	• high-frequency words

words that they often spell incorrectly. These can be chosen from any source. Have the student print the words legibly on small file cards. The cards should be kept in a conspicuous place for quick and easy reference. They could be taped to the student's desk or pencil case, kept in a writing folder, or put on their binder or notebook cover—anywhere that the student will be able to look up and see the words. Initially students may need reminders to look at the Demon Cards, but eventually their use will become a habit.

Demon Cards should be revisited occasionally to make sure they represent the current spelling demons. When a word is no longer misspelled regularly, it should be replaced with other words.

Cloze Encounters and High-Frequency Words

Using cloze passages in which high-frequency words are targeted provides a powerful means to reinforce spelling. Use text that is meaningful and related to the current themes or classroom culture. Blank out high-frequency words or parts of high-frequency words. As the passage is read, students supply the missing parts and provide a rationale for the suggestion.

Introducing and using cloze passages with high-frequency words. For a more detailed description, see Cloze Encounters pages 81–82. Various parts may be blanked out such as the following:

- whole words, which would focus on both spelling structures and meaning;

- everything except the first letter or blend, which provides a little more direction than blanking out the whole word;

- specific consonant or vowel clusters within the words, which draws attention to troublesome areas; and

- endings or prefixes.

Why use Cloze?	Skill Development
• It directs students to focus on high-frequency words within contextual language. • It helps to develop awareness of letter clusters or structures in these words. • It provides a chance for shared thinking about how the words may be remembered. • It is an activity in which all students can participate.	• high-frequency words • metacognition

Cloze passages shown on chart paper or on an overhead projection may be used effectively with the whole class. In this context, the teacher is able to monitor participation and call on all students. Students may have a copy of the passage at their desk to give them practice in repeated writing of the focus words.

Students may work in groups, but monitoring may be necessary to discourage more able spellers from simply providing the correct spelling. If the passage is completed with partners or in small groups, the less able speller may be assigned the job of secretary, thus ensuring them the opportunity to hear the correct letter sequence and to practice writing the words correctly. The passage may be started as a group activity and completed independently using the Word Bank as a reference.

Extended application. Students often enjoy creating a cloze passage for others. They may blank out parts of good copies of their own stories, notes, or reports. This activity provides good practice for students learning English to reinforce syntactic structures. Cloze passages can be used with all themes being studied.

Frequent-Word Sort

Sorting and classifying activities require children to focus on specific structures of words, creating or reinforcing both visual and auditory memory. In this activity, students are provided with a list of high-frequency words and are directed to sort the words into categories. The categories may be teacher directed or devised by the students.

Introducing and using sorting. For a more detailed description, see Sorting and Classifying on pages 82–83. Students should work in partners or small cooperative groups. They are provided with a list of high-frequency words. These may be the entire list that had been brainstormed previously or a selection from it. The list should contain about 20–30 words. Initially, students may sort the words into any categories that make sense to them. (They often come up with interesting categories that I would never think of.) As long as they name and explain the category, it is legitimate because it represents commonalties they have observed. The goal is to analyze the words to help them remember the spelling, so any analysis is beneficial.

Why use Sorting?	Skill Development
• It is an activity in which all children can participate. • It makes spelling manipulative—children are actually able to move words around. • It helps children become aware of visual and auditory structures of words. • It provides an opportunity for children to verbalize their observation about the words and to hear other students' ideas. • It reinforces that it is important to spell high-frequency words correctly.	• high-frequency words • metacognition

Extended application. A useful trick is to encourage the students to be flexible. Once they have sorted the words in one way, ask them to re-sort them into different categories. This encourages extended thinking. The teacher also may choose to direct the categories used, which could include common clusters, vowel sounds or clusters, length of words, number of syllables, or words with endings.

Orthography Lessons

Spelling is more than recognizing letter sequences or sounding out words. It requires the coordination of several sources of information. Orthography may be defined as the *art* of spelling; the expertise to coordinate and apply factual knowledge. The lessons in this section give students practice in refining this art. Guess My Thinking facilitates metacognitive awareness of a variety of strategies and the ability to choose the most appropriate. Adding Endings and Write a Picture develop mechanical knowledge and also the application of different word types to enhance written communication. Knowing when and how to use mnemonics to remember certain words saves many students from frustration.

Guess My Thinking

Guess My Thinking is a strategy that emphasizes that spelling makes sense. Volunteers share errors or successes and students try to guess the spelling strategies the volunteer used to attempt to spell the words. Students are encouraged to guess the thinking process their peers have used in spelling and, in doing so, they clarify and confirm their own awareness.

Introducing and using Guess My Thinking. This activity works best following a self-corrected spelling test or proofreading activity in which students have located errors. Prepare an overhead of the recording sheet using BLM 10. Brave volunteers are called on to share an error they made. This becomes easier as children become accustomed to the idea that their thinking is valued and that they will not be ridiculed for making mistakes. The error and corrected spelling are recorded in the first two boxes of the sheet. Volunteers are then called on to guess which spelling strategy had been used to

Why use Guess My Thinking?	Skill Development
• It reinforces that spelling is a thoughtful process.	• unusual or difficult words
• It structures a time for discussion directly related to developing metacognitive awareness.	• metacognition
• It provides a structured opportunity to share spelling processes.	
• It encourages children to think beyond using just one strategy.	

generate the attempt. Students should provide a rationale for their guess. The originator of the error is called on to confirm or deny the guess.

Extended application. This strategy can be used in many different contexts but should be modeled orally many times before being given as an independent or group assignment. Use is not limited to spelling. For example, during a science discussion, have students try to Guess the Thinking behind an opinion or answer given.

Guess My Thinking can be used as a group lesson at the overhead projector with the teacher or a Student Teacher recording volunteered ideas. Each student can complete their own sheet as the transparency is filled in. Errors may be shared and recorded as a large group, and the suspected strategy and reason could be completed in partnerships or small cooperative groups. Dividing the activity between large and small groups would emphasize discussion and participation. Each person in the group could share one word and have the group Guess Their Thinking.

This strategy helps students who are stuck in the phonetic stage to move on. They begin to realize that they must supplement phonics with other strategies.

Write a Picture

Write a Picture is an activity that links spelling and grammar. Following discussion about descriptive words, adverbs and adjectives, students examine a piece of writing to find examples of such words. Generalizations about the spelling of these words are described using the student-generated lists. The activity may include nouns and verbs as well.

Why use Write a Picture?	Skill Development
• It encourages students to focus on specific spelling structures as they relate to writing and word use. • It helps develop awareness of parts of speech • It builds the mental dictionary by extending known vocabulary.	• suffixes associated with adverbs and adjectives

Introducing and using Write a Picture. This activity should be done only after instruction in and discussion of how authors create pictures in the reader's mind using descriptive words. Students then can explore a piece of writing for examples of the parts of speech that have been presented using the questions in BLM 11. The words are written on the Write a Picture Chart (BLM 12). Once a number of words have been recorded, prompt questions encourage students to examine the words for spelling commonalties:

What do you notice about the adverbs? (*ly* ending)

Do all the adverbs have the same ending?

Is the same true for adjectives?

Are there any letter patterns with the adjectives?

Where are the adverbs and adjectives placed in relation to the word they are describing? Is this always true?

Their observations are recorded in their Spelling Logs. It is important to have students share their observations and conclusions and reflect on how this information can help them become better spellers.

Extended application. The words could be sorted into categories that reflect other spelling structures such as vowel sounds or syllables.

Clusters

Letter clusters refer to groups of letters that form a single unit of sound in English. Other terms that may be used to describe letter groups include phonemes, speech sounds; phonographs, letter symbols that stand for the sounds; consonant blends, two or three consonants blended with no vowel (for example *bl, gr,* and *str*); digraphs, consonant sounds that have no individual letter symbols (for example, *sh, wh,* and *ng*); and diphthongs, close blends of two vowel sounds (for example, *au, oo,* and *oi*). Clusters may have as few as two letters or may contain three or four. A list of common letter clusters and examples of each can be found in BLM 13.

Cluster Collection

Cluster Collection is a strategy that helps children develop an awareness of the common letter patterns of English and the frequency with which they will occur. Children need to know that even though the sound is appropriate, one would never write *kwick*. It is useful to know that *ight* is very common but never *ihgt*. How often will they find *ve* or *qu*? Sorting and classifying words found around them according to frequency of use will enhance discriminating awareness.

Introducing and using Cluster Collections. Working together as a whole group, ask students to brainstorm for groups of letters they think appear often in words. Record their ideas on a prelined sheet of acetate for the overhead (BLM 14). Although students will look at lists and charts in the room, do not have them search in books at this time, as this would distract them from thinking and trying to recall visually.

> *There are many questions to ask students when they are brainstorming for word clusters: What letter groups would never be found? Which ones are most common? Which clusters are longest? Which ones always go together?*

Why use Cluster Collections?	Skill Development
• They provide an alternative to attempting to isolate small sounds. • They help to make spelling predictable. • Good spellers tend to think in cluster parts rather than in individual, discrete sounds. • Clusters are presented in both the auditory and the visual mode. • Children become aware that some groups of letters appear in many words and that others such as *rla* never appear.	• high-frequency and difficult words • self-monitoring for accuracy • proofreading • long and short vowels • soft *c* and *g* • multisyllable words • prefixes and suffixes

Group the students into groups of three or four. Duplicate the transparency of brainstormed clusters and the recording sheet Cluster Collections (BLM 14) and give a copy to each group. Have the groups cut out the clusters and sort them into categories that indicate how often each particular group of letters would be found in English spelling: Never, Sometimes, or Frequently. A special category also has been included: Letters That *Always* Go Together. When the groups have completed the sorting, they should share the examples they chose for each category and their rationale for the selection. Discussion, followed by recording in Spelling Logs, should focus on what they noticed about different clusters and how this information can help them to become better spellers.

Letter Clusters

Letter Clusters is an activity in which students are encouraged to find occurrences of common letter clusters in stories or personal writing. By analyzing the letters and their use through a sorting and classifying activity, a deeper awareness of spelling structures will be developed.

Why use Letter Clusters?	Skill Development
• It explores the use of clusters in pragmatic writing. • It encourages students to become aware of spelling structures and generalizations. • It encourages students to inspect and think about letters that go together. • It facilitates metacognition.	• long and short vowel sounds • phonemic awareness • visual analysis • proofreading skills • high-frequency and difficult words

Introducing and using Letter Clusters. This activity may be used more than once, with a variety of themes or content units. The selected clusters may be taken from a story or article the class has read, from independent writing done by the students, or from brainstormed lists. Have the students work in groups of three or four. Tell them to choose clusters from the text. Depending on your focus, you may wish to direct the student choice; for example, find minimum length or multisyllable words. The clusters are recorded in the boxes on BLM 15, which are then cut and sorted into categories. Again, depending on the class and the goal of the lesson, you may wish to give guidance in selecting categories; for example, long vowels, suffixes, prefixes, one vowel, more than one vowel, or length of the cluster. The categories are to be shared with the large group along with the decision-making process.

Groups also are asked to share their observations and conclusions about the cluster categories. This may initially require guided questioning:

Did those clusters always say the vowel name?

Did any have more than one sound?

How did you decide which category to put it into?

Did you notice anything unusual about those clusters?

Discussion should be followed by a personal reflection in their Spelling Log.

Extended application. Selection could come from thematic words. This strategy means children focus on words they currently need for writing. Rather than isolating the cluster from the word, the words themselves could be sorted according to common clusters.

Error Analysis

Awareness of error patterns can give students direction in what to focus on when they are spelling; it also highlights particular areas that may cause difficulty, such as endings or homonyms. However, skill in error analysis often takes a good deal of practice to develop. The self-evaluation and extended thinking that result are worth the effort.

Beyond being fun, the activities listed here provide excellent practice opportunities in a number of areas including critical examination of writing and proofreading. Students need to apply orthographic knowledge to confirm their analysis, make corrections, and suggest areas for improvement. The challenge of putting thoughts into words is invaluable in confirming and clarifying understanding.

The process of analyzing errors and trying to find patterns should be modeled many times by the teacher and by Student Teachers. Exercises in error analysis should be done in partnerships or triads. This enables the less able speller to participate in a supportive situation. Identifying and fixing errors on their own, might prove to be very challenging for these students, but it can be fun in a supportive, nonthreatening group. Even if people find and correct all their errors, the less able spellers will benefit immeasurably from seeing and hearing their partners verbalize their thinking. More able spellers benefit too because the experience of putting their thoughts into words will help them remember. One generally remembers 90% of what one teaches.

It is imperative that many opportunities be provided to discover and share error patterns, through manipulating words, discussing observations, and classifying errors. If not, activities such as the Marking Guide (see pages 95–96) and the Writer's Report Card (see pages 96–97) could lead to frustration for both students and teacher. Some children may not be aware of appropriate or supportive language to give suggestions, yet they will maintain confidence and willingness to take risks in a supportive environment.

Data Collection

The Data Collection Sheet and the Data Reflection Sheet are places to record and classify errors and their corrections. They provide useful practice in awareness of error patterns. Students not only increase their knowledge of letter patterns, but they are encouraged to analyze their own spelling for evidence of repeated error patterns.

Introducing and using Data Collection and Reflection Sheets. Distribute copies of BLM 16 and BLM 17. Model their use on the overhead projector before they are used independently. Students then choose a piece of draft writing that they would like to analyze. They may work with partners,

<table>
<tr><td>

Why use the Data Collection and Reflection Sheets?
- They encourage attention to visual detail.
- They facilitate awareness of letter patterns.
- They provide practice in proofreading.
- They give children a chance to manipulate language.
- They facilitate metacognition.

</td><td>

Skill Development
- short vowel and complex letter clusters
- proofreading
- positive, effortful attitude

</td></tr>
</table>

especially if there are insufficient errors in one student's work. Students are directed to find and record in the boxes provided both errors and the correct spelling. The correct spelling is included so as not to reinforce a visual or tactile image of the error.

Boxes may be cut out and sorted into categories. It is important to name the categories, as this facilitates the awareness of similarities. For example, *figt* (fight), *thik* (think), and *comon* (common) are similar errors in that each word has omitted letters. *Cherreyes* (cherries), *playd* (played), and *runer* (runner) are similar in that the errors have to do with endings. Sharing and recording the various categories students generate extends and reinforces learning. The questions listed on the Reflection Sheet encourage students to extend their thinking in this area.

Marking Guide

Students love to mark assignments and to look for errors—especially if they are not their own mistakes. The Marking Guide is an application of an error-analysis strategy in which children read another child's story, locate errors, record their findings, and make suggestions for improvement. It is closely linked to the Data Collection Sheet on which students analyze their own writing for errors.

Introducing and using the Marking Guide. Distribute copies of BLM 18. Students should work in pairs or triads to ensure discussion. They are given a story to read in which they should locate any spelling mistakes. The stories may be their own, they may come from classmates who have volunteered their stories, or they may come from a different class, possibly a younger group. It is best to photocopy the stories, so as not to mark up the original.

<table>
<tr><td>

Why use the Marking Guide?
- It encourages attention to visual detail.
- It facilitates awareness of letter patterns.
- It provides practice in proofreading.
- It gives children a chance to manipulate language.
- It facilitates metacognition.

</td><td>

Skill Development
- short vowels
- complex letter clusters
- proofreading
- positive, effortful attitude

</td></tr>
</table>

Student markers are to look for patterns or similarities within the errors and record errors and the correct spelling in the boxes provided. This may be done visually for students who have had practice in this type of exercise. Less-experienced students may cut out the boxes and sort the words into groups. Students give suggestions for improving spelling to the author on the reflection sheet (BLM 19). These suggestions will show increased depth with continued practice. It is important to share good examples of suggestions with the whole class to model the appropriate language. The more real and truly useful this activity is perceived to be by the students, the more motivated and thoughtful they become.

Extended applications. Partners can exchange or work together to proofread each other's story. Photocopies of volunteers' stories can be made and distributed for practice. Older students can act as peer tutors for younger students.

Writer's Report Card

The Writer's Report Card (adapted from the work of Johnson & Johnson, 1987) is another variation of Student Teacher (see pages 79–81). Children assess and evaluate a piece of student writing and then write a report card for the author. As with all good teachers, they not only give a mark, but provide comments and suggestions for improvement.

Why use Writer's Report Card?	Skill Development
• It encourages attention to visual detail. • It facilitates awareness of letter patterns. • It provides practice in proofreading. • It gives children a chance to manipulate language. • It facilitates metacognition.	• short vowel and complex letter clusters • proofreading • positive, effortful attitude

Introducing and using the Writer's Report Card. Use this activity only after students are familiar with error patterns and types and the language used to describe the errors and to make positive suggestions. Facilitate success by using a transparency of the Writer's Report Card (BLM 20) on the overhead several times before students attempt to use it independently. See pages 29–30 and 39 for suggestions for error types on the Class Profile or Dictation Sheet.

Distribute copies of BLM 20 and give students a piece of writing to assess. The writing may be from the same sources as listed in the Marking Guide section earlier in the chapter. In the box labelled *Spelling Area*, the error type is listed. Types may be decided by individual Student Teachers as they read the article, or may be suggested by the class prior to starting the activity. Student Teachers decide on an appropriate mark for each category.

In the box labelled *Reason/Comment*, students provide justification for the grade (for example, C+: You had three long-vowel errors) or comments about noted patterns (Remember to change the *y* to *i*). It is usually helpful to list specific errors and to stress specific comments rather than just general statements. The *General Comments* area should reflect specific suggestions for improvement, including possible strategies and error patterns to watch for.

Which Witch Is Which? Homonyms

Homonyms are words that sound alike but have a different meaning. These tricky words do cause significant difficulty for many children, especially if the strategy used to learn them is rote memory. As adults, we tend to take most, if not all, homophones for granted. There is so much meaning attached to the word for us that we do not have to make a choice consciously. When we see a word or think about the spelling, the mental image created conveys meaning. This may not be true for many students. For example, the letters *w-i-t-c-h* create a picture of a crone in our mind, but children may not even know that there is another word with the same pronunciation.

> Many visual tricks can be used to help students remember confusing spellings: She is a *fri*end to the *end*.
> Let's go to get *her* to*gether*.
> Don't be*lie*ve a *lie*.
> Our *host* saw a g*host*!

Learning Through Use

Continued exposure to homophones within the context of written language will help to strengthen the associated meaning and automaticity that adults enjoy. As children read and write the words, they will have to think and make conscious choices less often, because the homophones will have become more automatically associated with meaning. In the context of natural reading and writing, structuring activities for students to hear peers describe their reasoning processes for remembering and deciding the correct spelling will develop competence and confidence.

Homonym Cloze

Homonym Cloze Passages have homonyms or parts of them blanked out to draw attention to their spelling structures. BLM 21, BLM 22 and 22A, and BLM 23 and 23A were written to support thematic units in my classroom. Although they are related to content we were studying, these passages were developed specifically to teach and draw attention to homophones. Working as a large group or in small cooperative groups, students share their ideas about how to fill in the missing letters. For a more detailed explanation of the cloze procedure see Cloze Encounters on page 81.

Introducing and using Homonym Passages. The passages are best introduced to the whole class using the overhead projector. Depending on students' familiarity with the procedure and with their concept of homophones, after the first paragraph or two they may be grouped into small groups to complete the story. It is not suggested that the stories be completed independently, as a significant contributing factor in developing success is the chance to talk and listen—to put one's own understanding into words and to hear other ideas. Following completion, group debriefing and individual recording of understandings in Spelling Logs will reinforce learning.

Why use Homonym Cloze Passages?	Skill Development
• They focus on a specific structure within the context of real language. • They generate an interest in language structures. • They structure an opportunity for students to share their strategies. • They provide an opportunity to play with language.	• homophones • metacognition

Semantic Lists

Success with homophones requires different spelling approaches. Attempting to spell them by sounding them out does not work very efficiently, because there is little if any difference in the sound. Homonyms *must* retain the semantic or meaning link for us to be able to make sense of them. For example, trying to remember the difference between *where* and *wear* is made much clearer when they are presented not as sound partners but with other words that have a similar meaning.

There, *here*, *where*, *somewhere*, and *everywhere* all have the same pattern; awareness of the *ere* cluster generates more memorable data than memorization by rote. Pattern awareness works for *weigh* and *way* or *wait* and *weight* if weigh(t) is related to another size word—*height*—both have the *eigh* cluster. *Two* may be associated with other number words such as *twenty* and *twice*, which at least eliminates one of the choices in *to*, *too*, *two*. The word *write* retains a visual and semantic association with the words *writing* and *written*.

Homonym Link-Ups

Link-Up Lists use the That Reminds Me spelling strategy (see pages 47–48) to develop success in the use of homophones. It creates connections among words containing similar letter clusters related to the meaning of the word. Key words are presented, and student groups must generate a list of words that are related to the focus word.

Introducing and using Link-Ups. Make an overhead transparency of BLM 24, Homonyms (and Their Link-Ups). Recall the That Reminds Me spelling strategy with the class. Discuss words that are often spelled in a similar fashion when their meaning is connected. Discuss how this knowledge can be used to help them to remember spelling homophones. Brainstorm words that have similar patterns based on meaning, for example, *medicine*, *medicinal*, *medicate*. Put these words in a list on the overhead. Present a homophone you have selected and have volunteers give words it reminds them of. Have them share why they think the words are related and how the similar patterns will reinforce the spelling.

Once the students are familiar with the process, have them work in groups of three to complete a copy of BLM 25, Link-Up Lists. Each group can either

There are many other Link-Ups:
for, fourth, four
(4 = our);
wood-would
(and could, should);
mussel, muscle
(muscular);
knew, know
(knowledge);
hear, heard (ear).
Many (but not all) of
the food related
partners contain *ea* as in
eat: pear, meat, steak,
bean, bread, cereal.

Why use Homonym Link-Ups?	Skill Development
• They help to make written language predictable by reinforcing visual patterns. • They provide a logical way to remember how to choose the correct spelling for homophones. • They reinforce knowledge about common letter clusters.	• knowledge about homophones • metacognition

work on one homophone and create a list and a presentation to teach the others, or each group can complete all words on a list you have provided. It is essential that the group's work be shared with the rest of the class. Posted lists will serve as reminders for students

Memory Tricks

Mnemonic devices are another way to remember these spelling demons as automatic competence increases. Indeed, many adults (myself included) still use these memory tricks to remember the spelling of their personal demon words. One problem with mnemonics is that they must have an internalized meaning to be of value, so just telling students your mnemonic trick may not work for them. Memory is enhanced only if the students are involved in generating and presenting the clue.

A copy of the mnemonics from Figure 10 on page 100 is included in the Black Line Masters for distribution to students (BLM 26). Have them add to the sheet and create their own memory devices Homonym Books.

Homonym Books

Homonym Books or posters are student-generated books or posters that present a mnemonic clue for remembering the homophone in a visual manner. These may be displayed in the classroom or compiled in a class book. The students are involved in creating the mnemonic as much as possible, although they may need some guidance or assistance.

Introducing and using Homonym Books Discuss the usefulness of mnemonic devices with the class. Share one or two of your personal favorites and ask for volunteers to share theirs. Tell the students they are going to cre-

Why use Homonym Blocks?	Skill Development
• They generate enthusiasm for language and shared thinking. • The visual aspects facilitate memory. • The memory clues provide a means to remember difficult words.	• homophones • metacognition

Figure 10 Mnemonics Are Memory Aids

A <u>piece</u> of <u>pie</u>

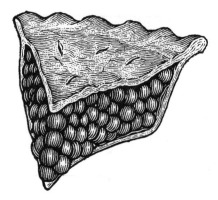

I h<u>ear</u> with my <u>ear</u>

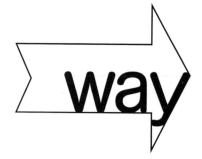

way

<u>Bears</u> have <u>ears</u>

witch

ate memory tricks to use with homophones, which will help them remember the spelling. Brainstorm a list of homophones. Students should be given the choice of working alone or with partners. Each student or partnership is assigned one group of sound-alike words for which they must create a mnemonic device. They are then to create a poster that presents the mnemonic in a visual manner that will make it memorable to others who look at it. Provide guidance at this point if students are having difficulty coming up with a drawing. The finished posters are presented to the class and may then be compiled in a class book or displayed in the classroom.

Hilarious Homonyms

Hilarious Homonyms are pairs of homonyms that create an amusing visual image. Students draw the picture that the pair suggests to them, and they share it with others.

Why use Hilarious Homonyms?	Skill Development
• They generate enthusiasm for language and shared thinking. • The visual aspects facilitate memory for homonyms. • They provide an engaging opportunity to focus on homonym pairs. • They create visual reminders of homonyms to post in the room.	• homophones • metacognition

Introducing and using Hilarious Homonyms. On the overhead, present a pair of homonyms that create an amusing image, such as *bored board*. Ask students to describe the mental image they get from reading the pair. Present another word pair (such as *bare bear*), but this time place the two words randomly or scattered on the overhead. Have students suggest the correct order to create the picture. Ask students to share how they differentiate the meanings of the words.

Present BLM 27. Have the students work with partners or small groups to draw pictures of the Hilarious Homonyms included in the boxes. In the empty boxes have them generate some of their own to share with others. Let the groups choose some of their favorites and create posters to put up in the classroom as visual reminders of homonyms.

Word Origin and Derivatives

The more fascination children develop with English words and language in general, the more likely they will be to remember the spelling of individual words. The origin of words and the ways in which they are related to or derived from other word draws students to learn about spelling. The more students delve into these connections, the more spelling begins to make sense; learning word origins therefore increases predictability. Roots or origins remain relatively stable as associated words are created. For example, *astronomy* and *astronaut* have the same origin based on meaning. Their spelling thus makes sense. For instance, students also enjoy the stories associated with some words. Knowing that the word *sandwich* comes from a lazy, gambling earl who could not even leave the gaming table to eat really peaks interest! A list of other interesting word origins is found in BLM 28.

Connections like these draw children into the study of language, sometimes in spite of themselves, and generate amazement and delight. In one class, a challenge to a very talented young speller to spell and explain the strategy for spelling the word *psychosomatic* prompted a week's worth of discovery learning for the whole class. The children pored over dictionaries, wrote out their word lists, and shared their ideas. Strangely enough, the challenged spellers were just as hooked as the strong ones. It was not difficult or threatening for them to look at words in the dictionary just like everyone else, or to make predictions. Although they may not have been able to pass a test on all of the words they looked up, they certainly acquired a great deal of visual and semantic information, and they felt good about their participation.

A number of lessons or activities have been included in this section that encourage children to make these connections and to expand their mental dictionaries. They are all related to using the Building Block spelling strategy introduced earlier (see pages 53–55). Once the Building Blocks spelling strategy, including the self-questioning component (Is there a part of this word I know? Can I make a new word by adding a part? What do I need to do to change it?) has been introduced, there is no sequential order to the lessons described here.

What's in a Name?

What's in a Name? is an activity in which students explore the spelling similarity related to the meaning of words that have foreign origins. The activity has three components and will probably last 2 or 3 days. By exploring the meaning of several words with common foreign elements, students will discover the meaning of the root.

Why use What's in a Name?	Skill Development
• It enables students to discover the spelling-meaning link. • It relates spelling to the meaning of the word. • It generates an interest and enthusiasm in learning unusual words. • It provides a more efficient strategy to apply abstract phonics knowledge. • It helps to expand vocabulary. • It helps students to be aware of manageable word parts.	• suffixes and prefixes • complex clusters • mental dictionary

Introducing and using What's in a Name? Distribute BLM 29. This activity should be done in cooperative groups of three or four students to facilitate conversation and shared ideas. Students sort and classify the words into categories related to derivation similarity. Encourage students to look for a common thread or meaning in the list of words with a common element.

After sorting the words, students should be encouraged to consult the dictionary to find the meaning associated with their derivatives. The meanings of the words provide a basis for predicting the meaning of the root. Groups should share their findings and their new insights into words and have a chance to hear other interpretations. Students may reflect in their Spelling Log or on the Reflection Sheet (BLM 30) using the prompt questions.

Some dictionaries have the foreign root listed. Students also can look up the words and find similar meanings.

Making Meaning

Making Meaning is an activity in which students explore the spelling-meaning link among words that have a similar origin. They are given a prompt word that has a Greek, Latin, or French base. By looking in the dictionary for other words that are spelled the same and comparing the meanings, they make the connection.

Why use Making Meaning?	Skill Development
• It makes spelling more predictable by relating the spelling to the meaning of the word. • It generates an interest and enthusiasm in spelling and a thoughtful, positive attitude. • It provides a more efficient strategy to apply abstract phonics knowledge. • It helps to expand vocabulary. • It helps students to be aware of manageable word parts in order to spell successfully, yet still retain contextual links.	• suffixes and prefixes • complex clusters • mental dictionary • strategy for learning unusual words

Introducing and using Making Meaning. Group students into cooperative groups of three or four. Tell them that they are going to do an activity that will help them understand why words are spelled the way they are. Distribute a copy of the Making Meaning activity sheet to each student (BLM 31). Choosing from the list of foreign origins in BLM 28, assign each group a key word that would be familiar. Each group should have a key word from a different word family. The key word is listed in the top of one of the boxes on the sheet

Groups are directed to search through the dictionary to find as many other examples of words that contain the same root. These are listed in the box below the key word. When sufficient words have been located, students are to discuss the meaning of the words they have found and decide how the words are similar and therefore predict the meaning of the foreign root. The suggested meaning is recorded in the box at the bottom of the list.

Each group reports their word list and definition to the rest of the class. This may be done by having students record their findings on a blank overhead of the Making Meaning sheet. As each group reports, the other students record the information on their sheet.

Reflection in Spelling Logs will help develop metacognition. Prompt questions that could be used are What did you learn by doing this activity? How will you be able to use this information? Can you think of any other words that you know that make more sense now?

Word Wheels

Word Wheels is an activity in which students create visual representations of words having a similar foreign word base. The base or word part is placed in the center of a wheel, and the derivatives are located and written in the spokes.

Why use Word Wheels?	Skill Development
• They make spelling more predictable by relating the spelling to the meaning of the word. • They generate an interest and enthusiasm in spelling. • They provide a more efficient strategy to apply abstract phonics knowledge. • They help to expand vocabulary. • They help students to be aware of manageable word parts in order to spell successfully, yet still retain contextual links.	• suffixes and prefixes • complex clusters • mental dictionary • strategy for learning unusual words

Introducing and using Word Wheels. Distribute a large circle to each student or to groups of two or three. If students are to complete their own wheel, they should be encouraged to work together to facilitate shared thinking and observation. The circle is folded in half three times to divide it into eight sections. The fold lines may be lined with a pen or marker for visibility, although a small circle should be left blank in the center of the circle

A key root word or word part is chosen or assigned and printed in the center of the circle. Using a dictionary or sharing knowledge, find related words and write one in each of the eight sections. Students add an illustration or sentence to reinforce meaning. As the Word Wheels are displayed in the classroom for reference, it is important to stress lettering, spelling, and visual appeal. When the Word Wheels are completed, they are to be presented to the class. Using BLM 32, students may copy the words from other groups' Word Wheels to keep in their Word Bank or Spelling Log. As usual, the activity should be followed by reflection and recording of new learning in the Spelling Log.

Word Origin Cloze

Cloze passages are activities in which letter clusters have been blanked out of passages of natural text. The blanks draw children's attention to the focus cluster and promote observation and direct instruction. The passages may be presented to the whole class, to small cooperative groups, or to individuals.

Why use Word Origin Cloze Passages?	Skill Development
• They make spelling more predictable by relating the spelling to the meaning of the word. • They generate an interest and enthusiasm in spelling. • They provide a more efficient strategy to apply abstract phonics knowledge. • They help to expand vocabulary. • They help students to be aware of manageable word parts in order to spell successfully, yet still retain contextual links.	• suffixes and prefixes • complex clusters • mental dictionary • strategy for learning unusual words

Introducing and using Word Origin cloze passages. Cloze passages used as class lessons to draw attention to word origins and derivatives by blanking out these word parts will give repeated practice and develop awareness. Content lessons such as science often provide text that contains examples of such words (for example, *astro*logy, *geo*logy, and *meta*morphosis). Have volunteers suggest spelling for the missing letters and provide their rationale for the suggestions. For more information about using cloze passages, review Cloze Encounters on page 81.

Adding Endings: A Mini-Unit

Adding Endings is a mini-unit created to encourage students to explore the intracacies of using affixes (prefixes and suffixes). It is a cluster of lessons that collectively help students develop an awareness of derivational words; learn about the rules of adding affixes, including an awareness of words and nonwords using affixes; and increase their ability to proofread critically. The goals were identified and activities were selected to guide student investigation (see Figure 11 on the following page). Unlike most of the other activities in this chapter, each activity included here builds on the concepts developed in the previous one. It was included to demonstrate how one might put together a longer unit of study using familiar teaching strategies.

In this mini-unit, students will explore the concept of adding affixes to create new words. They are essentially building a mental lexicon or dictionary. The rules for adding suffixes and prefixes are not presented for memorization. However, opportunities will be structured to ensure exposure and awareness for all students. They will observe, hear about, and verbalize

Figure 11 Goals of the Mini-Unit

This mini-unit will

- reinforce that endings are a necessary part of language. They affect the sound and meaning of a passage and are not simply rules to be memorized.
- facilitate the discovery of or extend the awareness of possible suffixes.
- teach or reinforce the concept of creating new words from known roots.
- teach or reinforce conventions about adding suffixes.
- structure opportunities for discussion and verbalization of the rationale for spellings and generalizations using suffixes.
- to provide opportunities for students to practice using semantic word analysis as a spelling strategy.
- reinforce the concept of self-questioning while spelling: Is there a part of this word that I know? Does this word sound right? Does it look right?

their own understandings of this complex skill in supportive, cooperative group activities.

These activities begin with a cloze passage, in which blanks have been created to highlight suffixes. From this, a collective list of known endings is generated. The Carousel Brainstorm activity that follows uses the list to brainstorm possible applications of endings to known words. Partners or triads proofread the brainstormed lists, sharing their collective knowledge and using outside sources such as dictionaries. The completed, amended list, including rationale and observations for selection and corrections, is presented to the rest of the group.

This unit may be completed over a period of five or six short (15- to 20-minute) lessons or in two or three larger blocks of time (40–60 minutes).

Introductory Activity: Cloze Passage

The purpose of this activity is to introduce the concept of adding endings within the context of meaningful language. Suffixes are necessary to make the story *sound right* and *make sense*, not because of what the rule says. The lesson provides an opportunity for students to access their prior knowledge about suffixes and to strengthen their ideas by putting their thinking into words. Hearing other children verbalize their thinking reinforces and teaches concepts and provides a window into the thinking processes of others. This activity is also an excellent chance for the teacher to assess the current level of knowledge and make instruction decisions. See pages 81–82 in the Cloze Encounters section of Chapter 6 for more discussion of cloze passages.

Remember that the goal is not to tell the students the rules about adding endings, but rather to encourage them to share their collective knowledge and to facilitate awareness and personal understanding.

BLM 33 is an article on tarantulas in which suffixes have been removed and only the root words remain. As students read through the article together, they can share their thinking about requisite changes to the words to have the story make sense. It is not necessary to use this particular passage; any thematic passage can be used.

After completing the cloze passage, students should fill in the reflection sheet. The list that is compiled from this part of the unit will be used in subsequent activities. Students are encouraged to reflect on and put into writing their current understandings of suffix generalizations. The goal of this activity is only for the students to access prior knowledge, not to make sure there are accurate rules written down.

Discovery Activity: Flower Power

In this activity students will explore word possibilities using suffixes and then analyze them for authenticity and correct spelling. In the first part of the activity, students will be working in teams of about five or six members. For the second part, they will return to their partnerships or triads.

Preparation. Group the students into teams of about five or six members. (The large groups will be split in half for the second part of the activity.) Prepare one overhead transparency and twice as many enlarged (11×17) copies of the flower (BLM 34) as there are groups. The copies are numbered and posted around the room in places where the groups may gather about them and write on them (for example, on the board or similar wall space). A large marker should be available at each poster.

Procedure. Using the model on the overhead projection, select a common root word and print it over the roots of the flower. Brainstorm new words created by adding suffixes to the root word. These new words are recorded on the leaves and petals of the flower. Remind the students that all suggestions are accepted and recorded during brainstorming. No judgment or evaluation of responses is allowed. This is a time to get as many ideas down as possible.

Carousel process. The carousel process begins with each group convening at one of the diagrams. A recorder is chosen or appointed in each group. Each group selects a root word and prints it on the roots of the flower. Possible root words might be *play, happy, help, clap, read, wish, comfort, silly, kind, drive, catch,* or *love.*

The groups are then timed and given 2 minutes to brainstorm and record all new words they can think of by adding suffixes to the displayed root word. The teacher's role during this time is to go to different groups and provide direction and prompting as needed. Encourage students to add more than one ending (for example, cheer-*ful-ness*). At the end of 2 minutes, the groups stop, put the markers down, and on the teacher's signal, proceed to the next poster. At the second poster, the groups are again timed for 2 minutes. They must read the words that have already been recorded and then brainstorm and record any new ones they can think of. This process is repeated about five or six times (gauge the repetitions according to the interest level of the group).

Analysis-Reflection Activity: Group Proofing

In this part of the mini-unit, students have the opportunity to make decisions about the correctness of the words they have brainstormed. This process further enhances the probability that they will internalize generalizations about suffixes. Rather than memorizing rules about isolated words, they will be creating personal meaning of contextual language.

Procedure. The students work in their original partnerships or triads. Each group receives one of the flower diagrams filled with the brainstormed words and a new, clean copy. They are directed to proofread the diagram and eliminate any words they believe are not correct. They should ask themselves a variety of questions: Is this a real word? Does it sound right? Does it look right? Is it spelled correctly? Students are strongly encouraged to consult a dictionary or other external source for confirmation, as mistakes are not allowed on their good copies. New words may be added if they know or discover any that are not on the list. The corrected list is printed on the clean copy, and students are given a chance to color the diagram to create a pleasing visual effect. Eliminated words and the reason for their elimination may be recorded on BLM 35, the Presentation Information sheet, to assist in the presentation or sharing stage. Students also should record their general observations about adding endings.

The word gardens and the information included on the sheet should be shared with the whole class. The Presentation Information sheet will serve as notes during class presentations.

It is important that students be given ample opportunity for reflection on the activity and their learning. The act of putting their thinking and observations into words will add clarity and facilitate personal understanding and future application.

Five-Minute Spelling Lessons

Teachable moments do arise naturally throughout the day, but I find myself not always able to take advantage of them. The impromptu moments do not always meet my agenda. I have, therefore, found it useful to plan and structure teachable moments to fill 5-minute blocks that occur during the day. The following suggestions are examples of useful, planned 5- to 10-minute spelling lessons. As with all other lessons, they are only suggestions and meant to be adapted and changed to meet different goals in different classrooms for different students. Many of them are games the children become familiar with and can be used with a variety of contexts.

Brainstormed Word-List Activities

Brainstormed word lists contain endless possibilities and have the benefit of being pragmatic language that has come from the students. If the words are on cards or strips, they have the advantage of being easy to manipulate.

ABC Order Cards. This activity develops visual analysis, frequently used words, and alphabetical order skills.

Keep a list of brainstormed words on cards and hand them out to students. Have them arrange themselves, or the cards, in alphabetical order according to the words. The rearranged cards can be mounted on a bulletin board for future reference.

List Cloze. This activity develops vowel- and complex-letter cluster and high-frequency word skills.

Present the brainstormed-word list with letter clusters blanked out either on the overhead or to partners or small groups. Have the students fill in the missing letters and share their rationale. It is not necessary to cover the original word to do this activity. Students who use the list as their strategy for filling in the letters will be developing a visual image of the correct spelling and will still be made aware of the focus cluster.

Impromptu "tests" or dictation. "Tests" or dictation can serve as guided practice in any skill area.

Use the brainstormed words in an impromptu spelling "test." Dictate a few of the words, have the children write them in their Spelling Logs, and then have them share the strategy they used to write each word. This can involve 1 or 2 words or as many as 10 to 20. It is a great way to fill 5 minutes before the bell rings.

Relay Games

Team games can provide the competition that some children enjoy without being threatening to others, as long as the emphasis is on team spirit and support.

Cluster Relay. This activity develops vowel- and complex-letter cluster skills. Some examples of clusters you can use are included in Figure 12.

Provide each team with a space on the chalkboard and print a target cluster in each space. The clusters for each team could be the same or different. On a signal, one player from each team races up and writes a word using the cluster, going to the end of the line when he or she is done. Suggestions and support from team members is to be encouraged. The goal is not to put unnecessary stress on individuals, but rather to facilitate an opportunity to develop awareness. Just by having teammates call the necessary letters from the sidelines, students have had auditory and visual exposure to spelling structures. The first team to complete a correctly spelled word for each member is the winner.

Figure 12 Example of Cluster Relay Words

Team 1	Team 2	Team 3	Team 4
ough	*ous*	*igh*	*ank*
enough	mouse	sigh	tank
tough	house	might	blank
rough	adventurous	flight	blanket

Letter Ladder. This activity develops vowel- and complex-cluster and mental dictionary skills.

A four- or five-letter word is written on the board for each team. Each player must race up and make a new word by changing only one letter of the word. Again, the first team to make a correctly spelled word for every player is the winner.

A variation of Letter Ladders is to have students change the original word into a specified target word. For example, change *line* into *said* in four changes. This variation takes planning on the teacher's part.

Example of a Letter Ladder	
Player 1:	cake
Player 2:	came
Player 3:	camp
Player 4:	lamp
Player 5:	limp

Make Words. This activity develops vowel- and complex-letter cluster skills.

Provide each team with a set of 20–30 clusters on small (2cm x 2cm) cards or pieces of paper. The clusters may be cut out by the students and moved around to form words. Another suggestion is to keep sets of cut up clusters in envelopes. The envelopes may be handed out quickly. Given a 2- to 5-minute time limit, teams are to make as many words as they can by putting clusters together. They are allowed to add no more than one letter to make each word.

Generic Activities

The following activities are not content specific and may be used repeatedly. The first three involve using personal or class writing to find application of language generalizations.

Check It Out. This activity can be adapted to develop any skill.

Present a rule or observation that someone has made or one that you want the children to explore. This could be from a cloze or proofreading activity. Direct students to look back in their writing (journals, notes, or stories) to find examples of words that either prove or disprove the rule. Students write the examples in their Spelling Logs so that they can be analyzed. It is much easier to make observations and conclusions from a comprehensive visual record than from scattered words found in writing or just heard. Give students a few minutes to look through their writing and then direct them to share as a group. From the words they have listed in their Logs, they should be able to make conclusions that have some basis in reality. List suggestions from each group on the board or overhead and reflect on the accuracy of their observations (see Figure 13).

Find Some…. This activity can also be adapted to develop any skill.

From a similar observation or prompt to those used in the Check It Out activity, have the children locate words in their personal writing that are examples of contractions, synonyms, homonyms, compound words, Greek or Latin roots, or whatever category you want them to practice. Share words that the children locate and any of their observations. This activity would follow instruction and practice in word origins.

Figure 13   Exceptions Using the Letter *C*

c followed by *e, i, y*	*c* alone
city	coat
receive	cheese
ceiling	crash
ice	could
dance	Cathy
police	call

Teacher: What did you notice about these words? Does the *c* say *s*?

Make a Rule. This activity can develop any skill area.

Using a cloze or other shared reading activity as a prompt, have students discuss and decide in small groups a rule for a specified structure. For example, ask students how they would decide whether to use *bl* or *ble* to make that sound. The student-generated rule should be copied into Spelling Logs and posted in the room for reference.

Student Teacher. Student Teacher, described in depth on pages 79–81, is an activity that children seem to enjoy and can be used whenever there is an extra 5 minutes. The Student Teachers can focus on practicing strategy use, explaining reasoning for spelling choices, directing games or relays, or dictating quick spelling "tests."

Conclusion

This chapter has presented methodologies useful for holistically developing the word knowledge necessary for spelling. We have now covered all three elements of successful spelling—attitude, skills, and word knowledge. Although the teaching strategies to develop these components have been discussed in various chapters they are not meant to be presented to children as separate entities. It is essential that they be interwoven and that overt connections be made with and for the students. Each lesson should have a metacognitive aspect to it to facilitate a positive attitude. For example, reference to and discussion about spelling strategies will be incorporated into Word-Study lessons. Bringing parents into the picture will enhance success even further. Chapter 8 will present some ideas for helping parents understand spelling development and enlisting their help.

The open discussion and investigative focus of the methodologies in *The Spelling Book* should establish a climate in which students are confident in taking risks and trying out their evolving theories about spelling words without fear of making mistakes. In such an environment, spelling growth will escalate with every writing event because engaging in consistent monitoring and reflection, rather than struggling to memorize rules, will lead to continual refining of personal understanding of the language.

As noted at the beginning of the book, I hope that you will use these lessons as starting points only. They are all meant to be flexible enough to be adapted to various content areas and adaptable enough to accommodate many different groups. It is not necessary to use all of the different lessons. If you find that some work particularly well for you, use them many times to teach several concepts. The repetition provides structure and security for some children. Remember there is no lock step, linear sequence to spelling development, therefore it is your professional judgment that guides the selection of lesson content. Your ongoing assessment and observations will indicate the teaching needs of the particular group you are working with.

8

Parents as Spelling Partners

s I discussed in Chapter 1, spelling causes concern for many parents probably because of the visibility of the errors. Spelling instruction that is integrated with other subject areas may not be obvious to parents. It is therefore critical when using this method of spelling instruction to assure parents that spelling is considered important. Parents often are accustomed to helping their children memorize spelling words. This has seemed to be an easy way for them to support their child's learning and success. But as our understanding of the spelling process has broadened, we have become aware that some of the methods that parents (and teachers) have used to help their children are not as effective as we believed. It has not been an easy transition for many teachers, and it will not be any less difficult for parents.

Parents Need Information

Parents' resistance to new methods in learning to spell usually stems more from a lack of understanding than from disagreement. It may seem to parents that whole language practices do not offer them any tangible way of helping their children. If we can provide clear activities that they can do to help students develop real spelling skills, then we will more likely feel support and commitment from them. Altering a parent's view of spelling may be challenging in some situations, but the results are worth the effort.

To effectively support spelling, parents need some general information about the development of spelling ability. Some information about development and a chart which outlines the natural stages that children go through have been provided in this chapter. Although it is not necessary for parents to understand the stages completely, it is helpful if they have some general conception about the progression of spelling knowledge. This helps them to understand their child's growth and suggests the types of strategies and knowledge to expect and emphasize at each stage.

Communication Matters

Good communication promotes support. Just the knowledge that there is a spelling program will ease the doubts of many parents and the more they understand the program the more their confidence will grow. Take every opportunity to share with parents what your class is doing to improve spelling and how you plan to organize your program. The sample letter to parents in Figure 15 on page 116 describing the principles of good spelling instruction may be adapted and shared with parents. Parent conferences provide perfect openings for discussion, but don't wait for formal occasions. Many classes have an informal "Meet the Teacher" evening early in the fall. Take the time to talk about your program goals and how you will teach spelling. However, it is not always easy to get the message across just by telling parents. You might find it useful to invite them to a demonstration of how to proofread or edit their children's writing. This could take place before or after school; some parents also might be able to come during the day while you are actually working with the class. You could even give them guided practice while they are there. Maybe they would even like to come back on a regular basis. Inviting those parents who are able to volunteer in the class not only gives them incredible insights into your program and great public relations, but gives your class an extra pair of ears for writing conferences as well.

Make sure parents are aware of the level of accuracy you expect on various types of assignments. Many parents believe that 100% accuracy is necessary on all assignments and do not understand the concept of draft writing. A written overview of accuracy expectations such as the one in Figure 14 may be sent home at the beginning of the year. Students should know the level of accuracy expected for homework tasks and be able to tell their parents. Encourage children to take their spelling dictation books home regularly to show their progression.

It is vital that the parents of students who struggle with spelling understand how you are trying to help their children. Problems can be exacerbated inadvertently if parents are unaware what to do. Parents want to help and often the only way they know is to drill on word lists. It is important to make the time to talk at length about how spelling evolves and the importance of strategy development. Help them understand that they use a variety of strategies and that they need to teach their children to do so as well.

Figure 14 Spelling Accuracy

Spelling is important, but it is not necessary to spell perfectly for all assignments. A good rule of thumb is the more people who will have to read the work, the more accurate the spelling needs to be. This table is a guide to the level of accuracy required for various tasks.

Please post this list at home for future reference.

Level of Accuracy	Description	Tasks
Ideas Only	• Spelling doesn't count.	• notes no one else needs to read • brainstorming • drafts of stories or reports
Readable	• Spelling should not interfere with reading the piece.	• thinking notes from class activities • reminder notes • lists • journals and learning logs • personal writing
High Quality	• Most high-frequency words should be spelled correctly. • Important concept words should be spelled correctly.	• class notes that will be used for studying • assignments that will be handed in for marking • research notes
Good Copy	• There should be no spelling mistakes.	• work that is to be "published" or displayed

Provide Parents With Spelling Tools

The chapter concludes with a list of suggestions for parents to use at home that may be useful. The activities are modeled on the kinds of techniques presented in this book so the child should be familiar with them. Encourage children to teach their parents. The ideas may be presented individually as specific suggestions for certain parents or be photocopied as a booklet to be sent home to provide general information for all parents. Some parents may find this long list overwhelming and would benefit from having you talk about the individual activities. You may choose to select only the most suitable ones for the child in question and send those home.

Suggestions to Give to Parents

Please note that the *you* or *your* in the two sections that follow refer to parents. Teachers may choose to photocopy this material and use it directly, or to adapt it to their needs.

Stages of Spelling Development

As children grow in their spelling competence, they progress naturally through developmental stages. In each of the stages, different cues and strate-

Figure 15 Letter to Parents

Dear Parents;

In Division ___ we think spelling is important, and we will be working hard to become good spellers even though we will not be studying for a weekly spelling test. Our spelling program may not look like yours did when you went to school, so I would like to tell you a little about the basic beliefs of our program and to assure you we do work hard on spelling.

- We believe that spelling is important in real writing. This is where we will spend most of our energies. We will learn about our language through many opportunities to proof-read actual writing, including how to locate and fix errors. Doing exercises does not ensure the development of good spellers.

- We believe it is important to know when to focus on spelling. Just like at home (for example, grocery lists, telephone messages, or notes), not all spelling needs to be perfect, so we will be selective in what we proofread. For example, only ideas are important in a draft copy, but a good copy should not have any spelling errors. Too much emphasis on correctness hinders development.

- We believe that it is important to learn a variety of spelling strategies. These strategies can be used to attempt to spell new words, which is more productive than to try to memorize the spelling of all the words we need to spell.

- We believe that it is important to learn about the structure (phonics, grammar, and letter patterns) of the English language. This is best done through group word study in which we explore words and share understandings of their structure rather than by memorizing rules.

- We believe that spelling is a part of the reading and writing process and should not be taught as isolated exercises. Isolated exercises eliminate the important link between meaning and application. The more spelling is used in real reading and writing the better the results will be. Spelling ability goes hand in hand with growing vocabularies and reading skills

- We believe in daily spelling activities. These are included within all of our studies so that they are more meaningful. For example, during a science lesson we might use our theme words to explore a certain letter pattern.

If you have any questions about our spelling program for the year, please do not hesitate to call and ask, or come in and we can talk about it. We welcome your input.

Yours truly,

gies are used to attempt new words. Very young children use squiggles and sticks to imitate writing and to convey messages. The messages cannot be read because they do not use any standard letter-sound matching. As children begin to understand this alphabetic principle, they use letter sound almost exclusively to write. They begin by using one letter to represent a word to increasingly complex phonics knowledge. Children gradually move past this overreliance on phonics and begin to use meaning-related cues to increase accuracy. These include things like adding endings or prefixes and understanding word families such as *sign, signature, signify, significant*. Sometimes children need a boost to get past the phonics stage into the meaning stage.

Figure 16 The Stages of Spelling Development

Prephonetic Stage

Children in this stage

- represent meaning or ideas with symbols.
- understand that writing represents a message (carries meaning for the author).
- write messages made up of random letters that cannot be read without interpretation by the author.
- are usually familiar with letters, but not sound.
- mimic the action of others.
- use a variety of symbols.
- show differences in meaning by varying the lines, order, or symbols they use.

Supportive Learning Activities

Parents can

- read to them often.
- have them write every day.
- demonstrate spelling—talk about it and help them develop *phonemic awareness* and *segmentation skills* (being able to hear the sounds in words such as rhyme or beginning sounds, being able to break words into parts).
- help them to develop the concept of a word and that words have a beginning, middle, and end.
- help them to develop letter-sound correspondence.
- develop left to right directionality.
- supply letters to play with.
- model writing for them.

Early Phonetic

Children in this stage

- begin to understand the alphabetic principle (that letters equal sounds).
- often use only surface features (the way the letter *name* sounds) of letters to spell. For example, *W* for *Y*, *C* for *S*, *G* for *J*, *Q* for *K*, *R* for *are*, and *LEFT* for *elephant* because that is the way the letter sounds.
- often use only a partial spelling of a word (1, 2, or 3 letters to represent a word).
- begin to grasp directionality.
- have a more complete knowledge of letters.
- may or may not be aware of, or segment, individual sounds in words.

Parents can

- draw attention to the sounds of letters rather than letter names.
- help them to develop awareness that there are more letters than syllables.
- continue to develop awareness and ability to segment (rhyme, initial, and final sounds).
- encourage them to experiment with invented spelling.
- help them to examine visual similarities in words.
- show them that they value their attempts at writing.

Phonetic Stage

Children in this stage

- represent words phonetically (only by sound).
- use systematic (often ingenious) inventions of spelling.
- spell what is heard with some sounds omitted or distorted.
- are generally able to segment and space.
- may have some sight words.
- may use vowels inaccurately.

Parents can

- help them to develop awareness of more complex letter clusters.
- help them to develop awareness of spelling patterns.
- increase awareness of syllables in words.
- increase awareness of irregular words.
- help them to develop awareness of prefixes and suffixes.

Transitional/Conventional Stage

Children in this stage

- are moving beyond just sound for spelling.
- incorporate visual strategies, word parts such as prefixes and suffixes, and word origins.
- understand that vowels are found in every syllable.
- are aware of common letter clusters.
- may use inaccurate sequences of letters.
- are aware that sounds can be represented in different ways.
- use an increasing number of sight words.

Parents can

- encourage them to observe, analyze, and discuss consistencies and patterns.
- provide opportunities to create and test their own rules or generalizations.
- encourage them to incorporate meaning, syntax, and origin to supplement phonics.
- talk about and share different forms of writing such as stories, reports, poetry, charts, and essays.

Figure 16 on the previous page outlines what spelling looks like at each stage and suggests the kinds of activities that are appropriate for each stage. It is important to be aware of this natural progression and to think of the types of activities that promote growth. For example, it would not make sense to try to expect a child to understand, or to try to teach them, about Latin root words if they were clearly in an early phonetic stage of development.

Supporting Spelling at Home

For some children, spelling may seem like a mystery. How does one remember demon words such as *to*, *too*, and *two*? How do you figure out *enough* or words with silent letters like *climb*? Children need to realize that our language really is quite predictable, even though it does not have a direct match among letters and sounds. We can help if we "share the secrets" (Scott & Siamon, 1994) of good spellers, teach the basic patterns of English, and help children to develop a confident and positive attitude to spelling.

The activities listed in Figure 17 on the pages that follow are techniques to support your child in developing his or her competence as a speller in meaningful and effective ways. They are designed to encourage the application of spelling skills in real writing and provide alternatives to simply having your child memorize a list of words. Your child's age and developmental spelling level as well as the task he or she is engaged in are the factors that will affect which activities you select. The activities may be used over and over, substituting new words, so choose the ones that best suit your situation. They are suggestions and are meant to be adapted to your home and your child. Above all remember to keep the activities enjoyable. Repetitive skill and drill will destroy motivation to learn.

As discussed earlier, three things are necessary for good spelling—a positive, confident attitude; strategies for trying to spell an unknown word; and knowledge of the language. The activities have been grouped in these categories. It is important to select some from each group.

Remember that the most useful way you can help your child to become a better, more thoughtful speller is to work with words in meaningful writing. Spend as much time as possible helping your child proofread his or her own work in a positive, supportive environment.

Spelling is important, but it is only one small component of total literacy development and school tasks. Keep it in perspective. Many poor spellers are very successful people. Work on spelling as part of other reading and writing homework or tasks, and do some specific word study game or activity perhaps once or twice a week.

Figure 17 Supporting Spelling at Home

Attitude

Talk openly and honestly with your child about when and why it is important to spell correctly.

Notes

Help your child to develop a spelling conscience by understanding that there are times when spelling is very important, such as on a job application or in a letter or report, but there are other times when spelling is not important, such as on your grocery list or in a first draft of a story.

Whenever possible, work with words found in your child's own writing.

It is essential that children get the message that spelling is most important as a tool for writing, not just to pass the test. Be sure and look at *all* their writing. This could include journals, creative stories, reports, notes, or diaries—anything that your child is willing to share.

Strategies

Have your child tell you how they figured out how to spell challenging words so that he or she develops the language to think and talk about his or her spelling.

Notes

It is very important for children to become aware of a variety of spelling strategies so they can make a thoughtful attempt at spelling a new word. This helps them to remember the strategies that work best for them.

Encourage your child to use invented spelling in draft writing.

Invented spelling is a child's independent attempt to write the letters that match the sounds heard in the new word. This encourages the child to try out what they are learning about the language. Research shows that children who use invented spelling develop word recognition and phonics skills faster than those who are not encouraged to spell the sounds they hear in words. This practice also develops confidence and independence. Children begin to realize they do have strategies they can use to spell a new word.

Help your child hear the separate sounds in words.

Read rhyming stories, play word games, clap the syllables of words, stretch out the word to emphasize the sounds, or make new words by changing the first sound. All of these activities that will help your child to discriminate the individual sounds—a skill necessary to effective spelling.

Find out how your child attempted to spell an incorrect word. You can do this by analyzing the spelling yourself or simply asking him or her.

Look at the error and ask yourself, Why did __ spell it like that? What were they thinking? This will help you to see that the errors really are built on thought and are not just careless mistakes. It will also help you to know what strategies your child finds most useful—what his or her learning style is. (Techniques include sounding out, finding little words, or remembering the way the word looks.)

As a first step in proofreading, have your child go through the writing and find as many words as he or she can that he or she is not sure about and would like to check.

Finding and fixing spelling mistakes seems overwhelming and difficult at first, but children really do improve with practice. Have your child go through the work, visually scanning each word. Professional proofreaders often go through the work backwards to eliminate the interference of meaning—children can try this too. Scanning helps build visual analysis skills and encourages independent proofreading.

(continued)

Figure 17 Supporting Spelling at Home (continued)

Strategies	Notes
Tell your child how you remember or figure out the problem word.	Share the strategies of an expert speller: Do you sound it out? Do you have a memory trick you remember? Do you think of a spelling rule or remember how the word looks?
When you spell a word with your child, encourage him or her to think of another word with the same or similar pattern.	Making these connections provides a memory link for making sense of the word and making it easier to remember. Jointly brainstorm words that have the same spelling pattern or word family. Post these word lists where the child can refer to them and reread them frequently.
Help your child to break larger words into smaller, more manageable parts.	This may just require reminders or more extensive help. If help is needed—first clap the number of beats in the word, then spell each part on its own. For example, *in-for-ma-tion.*
Give your child prompts to spell the word as needed.	Think of the last time you saw the word. Is there a part of the word you know? Is there a root word? Do you have to remember anything to add endings?
For words it is necessary to memorize, have your child say the letters out loud at the same time as they are written.	Some words really do not make sense, and we have to just remember them. Saying the letters out loud reinforces the auditory memory. Remind him or her to say the letters aloud as he or she tries to write the word in context.

Word Study	Notes
Teach your child to use a dictionary effectively.	Do not assume your child knows how to use a dictionary. Make sure he or she knows the alphabet sequence. Teach your child your strategies for looking up a word that has an irregular spelling (What does it start with? How else might it start?). Teach him/her how to identify and look up the root or base word and then to locate the derivatives.
Teach your child now to effectively use a spellchecker.	The computer is a wonderful writing tool, and the spellchecker is a valuable and legitimate spelling aid. Teach your child how to use it effectively. To use a spell checker as a teaching tool, activate the program. When it has highlighted the word, have your child identify the word part that needs to be changed or identify the correct word from the suggestions given by the computer. This helps to develop the visual analysis skill necessary for independent proofreading.
With your child, brainstorm a list of 50–100 (depending on age) frequently used words (words that your child uses all the time and that are worth remembering).	A list of high-frequency words is probably available from the teacher, although it is not as beneficial as one created by you and your child. Discuss the fact that these words are useful to remember, because we use them all the time. These are the words that your child will most likely be able to say do not look right.
Periodic practice with high-frequency words is beneficial. Talk with your child about why it is useful to remember these words.	Challenge your child to increase the number of these words he or she can spell automatically. Successful words can be added to his or her Word Bank, a list, word cards, or a graph drawn to provide a visual motivator.

(continued)

Figure 17 Supporting Spelling at Home (continued)

Word Study	Notes
Write the high-frequency or other target words on paper, but leave out groups of letters (*gr__ps, lett__s*). Have your child fill in the missing letters.	These cloze activities help your child to increase awareness of common letter patterns (an essential skill in spelling). For a change, have him or her make some cloze passages for you to fill in.
Keep a personal dictionary or Word Bank of misspelled or interesting words.	This booklet can be used to look up forgotten words, and it is a useful tool to compare similar words. Use Word Bank words when a list of words is needed for word-study activities. Keep your list of high-frequency words in the Word Bank. Add words from writing that your child asked you to spell.
Give your child periodic mini-spelling tests of the words worked on that day or words from their Word Banks.	Have the child mark his or her own test by comparing the word to the one in the Word Bank. Discuss how the errors were made—have him or her say what he or she might remember next time. Do not chastise for errors. Praise the effort and the words that were spelled correctly. Keep track by highlighting words consistently spelled correctly.
Help your child to remember the rules that are usually reliable. (Many of the traditional phonics rules are less than 60% reliable.)	Reliable rules include • basic punctuation rules including apostrophes for contractions and possessives, • *q* is followed by *u*, • every syllable needs a vowel, • soft *c* and *g* are followed by *e*, *i*, or *y*, • use *dge* after short vowels and *ge* after long vowels, • *i* usually comes before *e* except after *c* • for plurals, change the *y* to *i* and *f* to *v*, • use *le* at the end of words, not *el*, and • there are several letters we never put in pairs or partners such as *dj*.
Have your child do lots and lots and lots of purposeful writing.	The more real writing your child is engaged in, the more likely he or she is to improve his or her spelling. Purposeful writing tasks include diaries; letters to relatives, the editor, or Santa; shopping or to-do lists; stories; poems; captions for photo albums; notes to parents or siblings; instructions; recipes; or travel journals.
Play word games and do word puzzles.	Scrabble, Boggle, Hangman, crossword puzzles, word-search puzzles, and other word games provide a fun way to develop awareness of spelling patterns. These can be done either on paper or on a computer.
Put about 20 (depending on your child's age) words from a story or theme unit on cards, and together sort them into categories that have similar letter groups or sounds.	This sorting encourages both sight and sound analysis of words. Give each category a name and talk about the sounds of the words.

Spelling as Part of the Total Language Arts Program

Spelling is important. There is no denying that the ability to spell fluently is an asset, but it must be stressed that spelling should be viewed as one small component of a balanced literacy program. It should not be seen as an isolated skill to be drilled separately from literacy experiences, but should be interwoven through all the language-development activities that occur in the classroom. We want to make sure that transfer to real writing occurs.

We know that all the language processes are interrelated, interdependent, and reciprocal. What children learn about language in one area has impact in another by supporting, reinforcing, and enriching existing concepts. The more children make the connections from one context to another, the more pragmatic application will occur. We also know that the more actively engaged the student is, the more powerful the learning will be. Learning about language will not have the same impact as using language for real communicative purposes.

Another factor to consider in the language arts program is the weight to give spelling—especially in terms of marks or grades. Note in Figure 18 on the next page that spelling is a very small part of the big picture. It is a useful

Figure 18 The Total Language Arts Program

THE LANGUAGE ARTS PROGRAM

Oral Communication	Speaking	ideas	exchange of ideas and experiences
		awareness	strategies
			connection between listener and speaker
	Listening	physical	nonverbal cues
			voice
		language	word arrangement
			word choice
Communicating Information	Representing	structures	grammar
			spelling
		style	sentences
			words, figures of speech
	Writing	form	organizational rules
			variety of genre
		meaning	synthesis, detail, main idea
			power, engagement
Reading and Responding	Viewing	skills	word knowledge
			sound-symbol relations
		comprehension	literal
			inferential
	Reading	response to text	make connections
			synthesize ideas and information
		strategies	metacognition
			integrate cueing systems

tool for written communication, but not a necessity. One can function quite successfully and still be an abysmal speller. Do not overemphasize what is essentially one small subskill of one strand of the total program.

In *Spel is a Four-Letter Word* (1987), Richard Gentry uses the analogy of "kneeling on rice" (p. 7) to describe what learning to spell is like for some children and makes a plea for teachers and parents to "give them softer rice" (p. 7). In *The Spelling Book*, I have tried to outline an instructional approach that can ease the burden of learning to spell. The approach is more holistic than that of traditional spelling programs yet incorporates direct, planned instruction. Because there is no predetermined set of words to be learned by all students, the teaching techniques are intended to be flexible enough to support struggling spellers and challenge more competent spellers. The techniques are open ended and exploratory in nature and do not include lock-step, right-answer exercises. They thus are able to accommodate a greater range of diversity. Students can focus more on their personal strengths and needs. This philosophy moves spelling instruction from simplistic memorization exercises to training children in strategic processes relevant to developmental writing stages.

This approach refocuses the destructive debates in the field about *whether* to teach formal lessons, *whether* to teach phonics, *whether* to teach structure and grammar, *whether* to teach sight words, or *how* we help children learn these important concepts. Chapter 2 outlines research that has given us many insights into how children learn. We should be able to plan instruction to reflect these principles.

The Spelling Book attempts to address the factors that contribute to success as described in Chapter 3. (See BLM 36, the Spelling Program Assessment Checklist, for an outline of the principles on which the program is based.) These include intrinsic factors as well as behaviors and language knowledge. A climate for learning should be established that will support a positive, effortful attitude. This climate will facilitate metacognitive awareness, personal motivation, confidence, and risk taking, all of which are essential for student growth. The program provides direct instruction in the strategies used by good spellers, and students will learn the thinking processes that lead to success in standard spelling. Finally, students should be actively engaged in exploring and using written language to develop their knowledge of the patterns of the English language. Exploration occurs in meaningful contexts, and there will be extensive opportunities for students to see the processes modeled and to apply their growing knowledge through personal and crosscurricular writing.

Another learning principle that has been incorporated into lesson planning is that children learn at their own rate and in different ways. Effective instruction must accommodate the diversity. Children may become aware of a skill in one context, forget it in another, misapply it in another, and then revise their conceptualization before they reach a level of automaticity. It is the repeated experiences with using the words in a variety of meaningful contexts that enables children to explore and form their personal generalizations.

R E F E R E N C E S

Ball, E.W., & Blackman, B.A. (1991). Does phoneme awareness training in kindergarten make a difference in early word recognition and developmental spelling? *Reading Research Quarterly*, 26(1), 49–66.

Bean, W., & Bouffler, C. (1987). *Spell by writing.* Newtown, NSW: Primary English Teaching Association.

Beers, J.W., Beers, C.S., & Grant, K. (1977). The logic behind children's spelling. *The Elementary School Journal, 3*, 328–342.

Block, K., & Peskowitz, N.B. (1990). Metacognition in spelling: Using writing and reading to self-check spellings. *The Elementary School Journal*, 91(2), 151–164.

Borkowski, J.D., Day, D., Saenz, D., Dietmeyer, D., Estrada, T.M., & Groteluschen, A. (1992). Expanding the boundaries of cognitive interventions. In B.Y.L. Wong (Ed.), *Contemporary intervention research in learning disabilities: An international perspective* (pp. 1–21). NY: Springer-Verlag.

Brownlie, F., Close, S., & Wingren, L. (1990). *Tomorrow's classroom today: Strategies for creating active readers, writers, and thinkers.* Markham, ON: Pembroke.

Buchanan, E. (1989). *Spelling for whole language classrooms.* Winnipeg, MB: Whole Language Consultants.

Clymer, T. (1963). The utility of phonic generalizations in the primary grades. *The Reading Teacher, 16*, 252–258.

Cramer, R.L. (1969). The influence of phonic instruction on spelling achievement. *The Reading Teacher*, 22(6), 499–505.

Diakiw, J.Y. (1991, February 6). You can't learn to write by rote. *Toronto Globe and Mail*, p. 23.

Duffy, G.G., Roehler, L.R., & Herrmann, B. (1988). Modeling mental processes helps poor readers become strategic readers. *The Reading Teacher, 41*, 762–767.

Freppon, P.A., & Dahl, K.L. (1991). Learning about phonics in a whole language classroom. *Language Arts, 68*, 190–197.

Gable, R.A., Hendrickson, J.M., & Meeks, J.W. (1988). Assessing spelling errors of special needs children. *The Reading Teacher, 42*, 112–117.

Gentry, J.R. (1982). An analysis of developmental spelling in GNYS AT WRK. *The Reading Teacher, 36*, 192–200.

Gentry, J.R., (1987). *Spel is a four-letter word.* Richmond Hill, ON: Scholastic-TAB.

Gentry, J.R., & Gillet, J.W. (1993). *Teaching kids to spell.* Portsmouth, NH: Heinemann.

Goodman, K., (1986). *What's whole in whole language?* Richmond Hill, ON: Scholastic-TAB.

Goodman, Y.K., Watson, D.J., & Burke, C.L. (1987). *Reading miscue inventory.* Katonah, NY: Richard C. Owen.

Graham, S., & Miller, L. (1979). Spelling research and practice: A unified approach. *Focus on Exceptional Children, 12*(2), 1–16.

Graves, D.H. (1976). Research update: Spelling tests and structural analysis methods. *Language Arts, 54*, 86–90.

Groff, P. (1979). Phonics for spelling. *The Elementary School Journal, 79*, 269–275.

Groff, P. (1986). The implications of developmental spelling research: A dissenting view. *The Elementary School Journal*, 86(3), 317–323

Henderson, E.H. (1981). *Learning to read and spell.* DeKalb, IL: Northern Illinois University Press.

Henderson, E.H., & Templeton, S. (1986). A developmental perspective of formal spelling instruction through alphabet, pattern, and meaning. *The Elementary School Journal, 86*(3), 305–316

Hillerich, R.L. (1982). That's teaching spelling??? *Educational Leadership, 39,* 615–617.

Johnson, T.D., & Johnson, I.L. (1987). *Literacy through literature.* Toronto, ON: Scholastic.

McCracken, R.A., & McCracken, M.J. (1985). *Spelling through phonics.* Winnipeg, MB: Peguis.

Lie, A. (1991). The effects of a training program for stimulating skills in word analysis in first-grade children. *Reading Research Quarterly, 6,* 234–250.

Palincsar, A.S., & Ransom, K. (1988). From the mystery spot to the thoughtful spot: The instruction of metacognitive strategies. *The Reading Teacher, 41,* 784–789

Paris, S.G., & Jacobs, J. (1984). The benefits of informed instruction for children's reading awareness and comprehension skills. *Child Development, 5*(5), 2083–2093.

Paris, S.G., Lipson, M.Y., & Wixson, K.K. (1983). Becoming a strategic reader. *Contemporary Educational Psychology, 8,* 293–316.

Personke, D. & Yee, A. (1971). *Comprehensive spelling instruction: Theory, research, and application.* Scranton, PA: Intertext.

Radebaugh, M.R. (1985). Children's perceptions of their spelling strategies. *The Reading Teacher, 38,* 532–536.

Rosencrans, G. (1993). *The effects of direct instruction within a whole language spelling program.* Unpublished master's thesis, Simon Fraser University, Vancouver, Canada.

Rule, R. (1982). The spelling process: A look at strategies. *Language Arts, 59*(4), 379–384.

Santa, C. (Ed.). (1996). *Creating independence through student-owned strategies* (2nd ed.). Dubuque, IA: Kendall-Hunt.

Scott, J., (1991). Guidelines for vocabulary instruction: Extending current theory to students with special needs. *Exceptionality Education Canada, 1*(3), 27–43.

Scott, J., Hiebert, E., & Anderson, R. (1992). Research as we approach the millennium: Beyond becoming a nation of readers. In F. Lehr & J. Osborn (Eds.), *Reading, language, and literacy: Instruction for the twenty-first century.* (pp. 253–280). Hillsdale, NJ: Erlbaum.

Scott, R. (1990). Whole language and spelling: Perspectives from teachers, parents and administrators. *Orbit, 21*(4), 1.

Scott, R., & Siamon, S. (1994). *Sharing the secrets: Teach your child to spell.* Toronto, ON: Macmillan.

Simon, D.P., & Simon, H.A. (1973). Alternative uses of phonemic information in spelling. *Review of Educational Research, 43*(1), 115–137

Slavin, R.E. (1987). Cooperative learning and the cooperative school. *Educational Leadership, 45,* 7–13.

Slavin, R.E. (1991). Synthesis of research on cooperative learning. *Educational Leadership, 48,* 71–82.

Stahl, S.A., (1992). Saying the p word: Guidelines for exemplary phonic instruction. *The Reading Teacher, 45*(8), 618–625.

Stanovich, K. (1994). Romance and reality. *The Reading Teacher, 47,* 280–291.

Swanson, H.L. (1989). Strategy instruction: Overview of principles and procedures for effective use. *Learning Disabilities Quarterly, 12,* 3–14.

Tarasoff, M. (1990). *Spelling strategies you can teach.* Victoria, BC: Pixelart Graphics.

Tarasoff, M. (1992). *A guide to children's spelling development for parents and teachers.* Victoria, BC: Active Learning Institute.

Templeton, S. (1979). Spell first, sound later. *Research in the Teaching of English, 13*(3); 255–264.

Templeton, S. (1986). Synthesis of research on learning and teaching spelling. *Educational Leadership, 13*(6), 73–78.

Thomas, V. (1979). *Teaching spelling: Canadian word lists and instructional techniques.* Toronto, ON: Gage.

Thomas, V., & Braun, C. (1979). *The Canadian spelling program: Teacher's edition.* Toronto, ON: Gage.

Villa, R.A., & Thousand, J.S. (1988). Enhancing success in heterogeneous schools: The powers of partnerships. *Teacher Education and Special Education, 11*(4), 144–154.

Wade, S.E., & Reynolds, R.W. (1989). Developing metacognitive awareness. *Journal of Reading, 33,* 6–14.

Weinstein, C.E., (1987). Fostering learning autonomy through the use of learning strategies. *Journal of Reading, 30,* 590–595.

Wong, B.Y.L. (1986). A cognitive approach to teaching spelling. *Exceptional Children, 53*(2), 169–173.

Wong, B.Y.L. (1992). On cognitive process-based instruction: An introduction. *Journal of Learning Disabilities, 25*(3), 150–152.

Yong, F.L., & McIntyre, J.D. (1992). A comparative study of learning style preferences of students with learning disabilities and students who are gifted. *Journal of Learning Disabilities, 25*(2), 124–132.

Yopp, H.K. (1992). Developing phonemic awareness in young children. *The Reading Teacher, 45,* 696–703.

INDEX

L

LANGUAGE ARTS PROGRAM, 123–125, 124*f*; spelling as part of, 123–125

LEARNERS: developmental levels of, 6

LEARNING: assumptions about, 6–7; cooperative, 12, 33–34; expected outcomes, 23, 24*f*; observation and, 12–13; as social process, 7; stages of, 13–15; supportive activities, 117*f*; through use, 97

LEARNING ACTIVITIES. *See* Activities

LEARNING OUTCOMES LIST, 67

LEHR, F., 128

LESSONS, 30–35; for Error Analysis, 94–97; five-minute, 86, 86*f*, 108–111; for frequently used words, 87–90; generic, 76; goals for, 30, 31*f*; orthography, 90–92; rule for, 32; sample weeks of, 40, 41*f*; specific, 86, 86*f*; whole-group, 32–33; word origin and derivatives, 101–105; word-study, 8, 85–111. *See also* Activities; Strategies

LETTER CLUSTERS, 86*f*, 93–94; extended application, 94; goals, 31*f*; guided questioning for, 93; introducing and using, 93–94; why to use, 93

LETTER LADDER, 47, 86*f*, 109; example ladder, 109; goals, 31*f*; variation, 110

LETTERS TO PARENTS, 114, 116*f*

LIE, 17, 26

LINK-UPS, 98; goals, 31*f*; homonym, 86*f*, 98–99; introducing and using, 98–99

LIPSON, M.Y., 46, 128

LIST CLOZE, 86*f*, 108–109; goals, 31*f*

LISTS: brainstormed word-list activities, 108–109; frequent-word, 31*f*, 74; most frequently written words, 87; semantic, 86*f*, 98; word, 74–75

LOGS, 8, 35–36, 39; goals, 31*f*; introducing, 75; prompts for, 35, 36*f*; reflection on thinking and understanding in, 62

LOOKING GOOD, 48–49, 55; goals, 31*f*; how to introduce and use, 48–49; suggestions for using, 49; why to use, 48

M–N

MAKE A RULE, 86*f*, 111; goals, 31*f*

MAKE WORDS, 86*f*, 110; goals, 31*f*

MAKING MEANING, 86*f*, 103–104; goals, 31*f*; introducing and using, 103–104; why to use, 103

MANAGEMENT STRATEGIES, 29–30

MANAGER (JOB), 34

MARKING GUIDE, 86*f*, 94, 95–96; extended applications, 96; goals, 31*f*; introducing and using, 95–96; why to use, 95

MCCRACKEN, M.J., 5, 128

MCCRACKEN, R.A., 5, 128

MCINTYRE, J.D., 26, 128

MEANING: Making Meaning, 31*f*, 86*f*, 103–104; studying, 28

MECHANICS, 78

MEEKS, J.W., 19, 127

MEMORIZATION, 15–16

BLACK LINE MASTERS

The Black Line Masters (BLMs) are for your use in teaching the lessons found in *The Spelling Book*. The numbers at the top of each page correspond to the numbers in the text. They may be reproduced freely for class distribution, as long as the credit line at the bottom appears on each copy.

Although there are no page numbers on the BLMs, they appear in the order to which they are referred in the text of the book.

BLM 1 Expected Learning Outcomes in Spelling

Students will	Early Primary		Primary/Intermediate		Intermediate
	Pre-phonetic	Phonic	Grapho-phonic	Ortho-phonic	Morpho-phonic
Attitudes					
recognize the contexts in which spelling is important					
develop a positive, effortful attitude					
develop a spelling conscience					
develop an interest in words and spelling					
Skills					
learn to spell a variety of words frequently used in writing					
learn strategies applicable to spelling a variety of words					
apply spelling strategies in all writing activities					
monitor the accuracy of spelling while writing					
develop skills in proofreading					
develop strategies for learning and retaining the spelling of unusual or difficult words					
develop a mental dictionary (extend knowledge of one word to spell another)					
be able to verbalize effective spelling strategies and their application (metacognition)					
develop visual analysis skills					
predict spelling based on meaning					
Knowledge					
increase understanding of written words conveying meaning					
initial consonants					
final consonants					
medial consonants					
spacing between words					
consonant blends					
short vowel clusters (*at*, *ash*, and *ent*)					
regular double vowels (*ee*, *ea*, and *ie*)					
vowel clusters (*ou*, *oi*, *ow*, and *au*)					
'soft' *c* and *g*					
possessives					
complex clusters (*ough*, *tion*, and *igh*)					
multisyllable words					
punctuation					
capital letters					
plurals					
abbreviations					
contractions					
prefixes					
simple suffixes (*ed*, *ing*, and *er*)					
homonyms					
word origins (French, Greek, and Latin)					
derivatives (*ness*, *ly*, and *tion*)					

BLM 2 Class Spelling Profile

	Consonants	Short vowels (at, ith, and op)	Vowel clusters (ee, oa, ow, and au)	Complex clusters (ough, tion, and igh)	Punctuation	Prefixes/Suffixes	Homonyms	Derivatives (ness, ly, and tion)	Word Origins (Greek, Latin, and French)

Black Line Master 2 Class Spelling Profile. *The Spelling Book: Teaching Children How to Spell, Not What to Spell* by Gladys Rosencrans, ©1998. Newark, DE: International Reading Association. May be copied.

BLM 3 Spelling Dictation

Date _____

Test	Correction	Saying Word	Short Vowels	Long Vowels	Clusters	Endings	Reversals	Omissions

Date _____

Test	Correction	Saying Word	Short Vowels	Long Vowels	Clusters	Endings	Reversals	Omissions

To fix an error, keep the parts of the word that you are sure are right and only change those parts you are not sure of. Write your changes in the boxes and pick the one that looks the best.

Miscue	First Change Keep what you are sure is right	Second Change What else is possible?	Third Change Is anything else possible?	Standard Spelling

Name _____

Date _____

1. Is it important to learn how to spell? Why?

2. When you are writing a story draft or writing in your journal, how do you spell words you don't know?

3. What do you do when you come to a word you don't know how to spell?
   Do you ever do anything else?

4. What is the most important thing to remember about spelling?

5. Who helped you the most to learn to spell?
   How did they help?

6. How do you find the mistakes in a draft?
   What do you do to change them to the correct spelling?

7. What is the hardest part of spelling?

8. How would you teach a young person to spell?

9. What would you like to learn or do better this year in spelling?

10. Are you a good speller? Why or why not?

Rate the following strategies. How often do you use them to spell words when you are writing a story, a report, or in your journal?

Sound out the word	not very often	sometimes	most of the time
Think about how it looks	not very often	sometimes	most of the time
Look it up in a dictionary	not very often	sometimes	most of the time
Find the word in a list or book	not very often	sometimes	most of the time
Ask a friend or teacher	not very often	sometimes	most of the time

Name _____

Date _____

1. Spelling is important because...

2. When I am writing a story draft or in my journal, I spell words by...

3. When I come to a word I'm not sure how to spell, I...
    Sometimes I also...

4. The most important thing to remember about spelling is...

5. _____ helped me the most to learn to spell. They helped by...

6. The hardest thing about spelling is...

7. When I am writing a good copy of a story or report, I find the errors by...

8. I change them to the correct spelling by...

9. To teach a young person to spell, I would...

10. The most important thing I learned in spelling this year was...

11. I am/am not a good speller because...

Rate the following strategies. How often do you use them to spell words when you are writing a story, a report, or in your journal?

Sound out the word	not very often	sometimes	most of the time
Think about how it looks	not very often	sometimes	most of the time
Look it up in a dictionary	not very often	sometimes	most of the time
Find the word in a list or book	not very often	sometimes	most of the time
Ask a friend or teacher	not very often	sometimes	most of the time
Look up the word in my Word Bank	not very often	sometimes	most of the time
SIP	not very often	sometimes	most of the time
ICE	not very often	sometimes	most of the time
RAP	not very often	sometimes	most of the time
Building Blocks	not very often	sometimes	most of the time
Looking Good	not very often	sometimes	most of the time
That Reminds Me	not very often	sometimes	most of the time

Name _____

Assignment _____ Date _____

	Misspellings	Total
Phonetic (pronunciation)		
Phonic (sound symbol) consonants/blends		
short vowel clusters (*an*, *ish*, and *ent*)		
long vowels (*ee*, *oa*, *ei*, and *y*)		
vowel clusters (*oi*, *aw*, *ou*, and *or*)		
complex clusters (*tion*, *ough*, and *ight*)		
Semantic (meaning) prefixes/suffixes		
punctuation/capitals		
homonyms		
contractions		
origins/derivatives (French and Greek) (*ness*, *ly*, and *tion*)		
Omissions		
Reversals		
Standard Spellings Noted		

Total # of words _____   percentage accuracy _____

BLM 8 Spelling Behaviors Checklist

Does the student:	usually	at times	seldom
show a positive, thoughtful attitude?			
know when/where spelling is important?			
show a willingness to attempt new words independently?			
use a variety of spelling strategies in writing?			
verbalize his or her spelling strategies?			
correctly segment words for spelling?			
use basic sound-symbol relations?			
use a varied and extensive speaking vocabulary?			
demonstrate ability to paraphrase word knowledge?			
use age-appropriate, specialized language in writing?			
consistently spell age-appropriate high-frequency words correctly?			
use grammatical structures correctly?			
maintain and use a Word Bank?			
write in a variety of genre?			
know how to use a dictionary?			
use a thesaurus effectively?			
demonstrate knowledge of common letter clusters?			
demonstrate knowledge of contractions?			
demonstrate knowledge of homophones?			
demonstrate knowledge of prefixes and suffixes?			
demonstrate ability to find errors in writing?			
demonstrate ability to correct errors in writing?			

Notes:

Theme _____

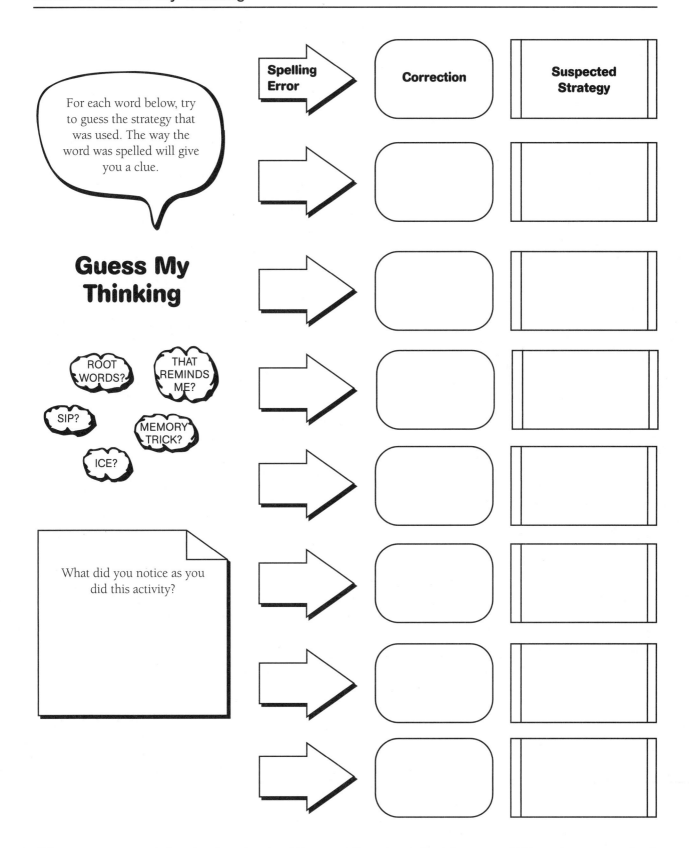

For each word below, try to guess the strategy that was used. The way the word was spelled will give you a clue.

Guess My Thinking

ROOT WORDS?

THAT REMINDS ME?

SIP?

MEMORY TRICK?

ICE?

What did you notice as you did this activity?

Spelling Error

Correction

Suspected Strategy

Just like cameras, words can create effective pictures.

Interesting naming and action words (**nouns** and **verbs**) can create pictures in the mind's eye. These pictures are brought further into focus by using words that describe the naming and action words. These words are called **adjectives** and **adverbs**.

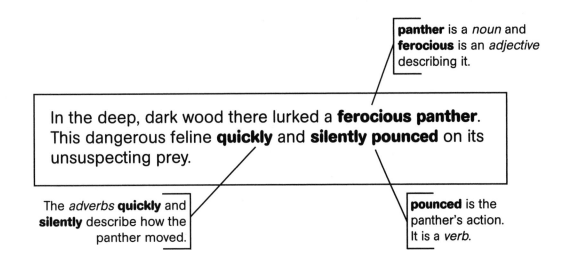

panther is a *noun* and **ferocious** is an *adjective* describing it.

In the deep, dark wood there lurked a **ferocious panther**. This dangerous feline **quickly** and **silently pounced** on its unsuspecting prey.

The *adverbs* **quickly** and **silently** describe how the panther moved.

pounced is the panther's action. It is a *verb*.

Do the following activities with a partner. Share your ideas.

1. Use the chart to record your words.

2. Look back at the selection you have just read and find interesting examples of *nouns* and *verbs* that help to create pictures. List these in the appropriate columns.

3. Now find all the *adjectives* and *adverbs* from the selection and list them as well.

4. What did you notice about the adverbs?

5. Is the same true for adjectives?

6. Write your observations in your Spelling Log.

7. Check with other students and see what they noticed.

Optional:

1. Add other words you can think of to the list of adjectives. Check with friends and keep adding words until you have 20–25.

2. Sort your list of adjectives into categories that go together. Remember to give each category a name.

3. Share your categories with the class and compare category names. Did anyone have one that surprised you?

4. In your Spelling Log, write in your own words what you have learned about *parts of speech* (nouns, verbs, adjectives and adverbs).

Name _____

Story _____ Date _____

NOUNS	VERBS	ADVERBS	ADJECTIVES

BLM 13 Some Useful Letter Clusters

at	as	ad	an	am	ar
ain	ask	ack	are	and	ant
ed	en	et	em	ep	eg
ent	ept	est	eld	ell	er
is	ig	ip	in	im	it
ing	ink	ish	ind	itch	ill
og	ot	op	on	ob	or
ost	ong	oll	ond	ock	
un	ug	ut	up	us	ur
uck	ung	ulk	uch	ull	ush
cr	br	cl	pl	dr	gr
sp	st	tr	fr	fl	sh
mp	nd	nt	sk	sl	th
ame	ade	ake	ave	ace	ay
ail	ait	age	air	arp	art
arm	ard	ark	arge	arch	
ee	eet	eel	eep	eat	eat
ead	ear	eam	andy	any	ancy
ime	ide	ike	ive	ine	ire
igh	ight	ind	ild	irt	ird
ule	ure	ume	use	uge	ute
ew	oo				
ome	obe	oke	ose	one	ope
oat	oast	ow	old	ost	oal
orn	orse	ork	orch	ort	oin
alf	kn	wr	tle	kle	mb
gle	ble	ple			
tion	ight	ure	ness	ious	ment
age	less	able	ough	each	

BLM 14 Cluster Collection

Name _____

Date _____

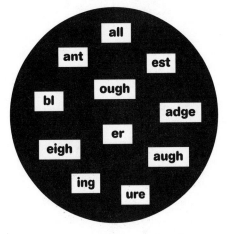

Letters that **Never** Go Together	Letters that **Sometimes** Go Together	Letters that **Frequently** Go Together	Letters that **Always** Go Together

From the story you have just read look for groups of letters that are often found together. We call these *letter clusters*. Fill in as many boxes in the chart below as you can.

1. Think about how these clusters are used: • in words • for spelling • how they look • how they sound • other ideas

2. Cut out the clusters and sort them into groups or categories according to how you think they go together. Make sure you name each category! Be prepared to share your group's thinking with the class.

3. In your Spelling Log think about these questions:

   • What are your observations about how letter clusters are used in spelling words.

   • Do some clusters usually come at the end (or beginning) of words? Which ones?

   • Are any clusters spelled differently than they sound?

   • Are you surprised about any of the clusters? Which ones?

   • What have you learned that will make you a better speller?

DATA COLLECTION SHEET

- Go through some of your draft writing and look for spelling errors.
- List the errors in the boxes below.
- Make sure to put the correct spelling beside the incorrect one. A sample has been done for you.
- Make sure your writing in the boxes is legible!

hav	have						

Name _____

Writing Used _____ Date _____

What was your most common
error type?

What spelling surprised you?

What will you remember next
time you are writing?

DATA
REFLECTION
SHEET

What one(s) made you say
"Oh no! How could I have done that?"
Why?

What were
some vowel
errors?

peopl	people				

Student Teacher(s) _____

Assignment _____ Date _____

Go through the student's work and look for spelling errors. List the errors in the boxes on the Marking Sheet so you can analyze them. Give suggestions to the student about how to improve his or her spelling. Think about the following questions.

Make sure to put the correct spelling beside the incorrect one. One has been done for you.

Were any of the errors similar? Which ones?

What strategy do you think the student used the most?
Would you recommend a different one? Which one? Why?

What suggestions would you give the student to help him or her be a better speller?

From a current sample of writing, analyze and give a mark for the following areas of spelling.

Remember: You must be able to give reasons for the mark.

Give specific comments.

A   Excellent
B   Very good
C+ Above average
C   Good
D   Needs work

Spelling Area	Mark	Reason/Comment

General Comments: Comment on how this student could become a better speller.

Signature: _____

Bobby Bear at the Fair

Last w_____ Bobby B_____ went to a f_____ in the country. His cousin had

s_____ him the train f_____ to get th_____.

When he got th_____ he h_____ a loud noise and ran to s_____ what it was. "I

think it is a h_____ of elephants!" he thought.

"No. It is just the band I can h_____," he realized when he got to the big tent.

He walked around the f_____ and looked at all the people. As he w_____ted to

go f_____ a ride on the Ferris wheel, he saw a crowd at a booth. "Th_____ is the

Fortune Teller," he thought, "I wonder if she could guess my w_____t and height.

Maybe I w_____d win a f_____ry, stuffed animal!"

Bobby felt hungry, so he went to the food tent. He got a bowl of ch_____ for

f_____ty cents and t_____ p_____s for a dime. He got e_____t p_____ces of

chocolate to share with his cousin t_____.

As he a_____ his lunch he saw his cousin come th_____ the gate. "H_____

Jeremiah! H_____ I am. Come over h_____. Can you h_____ me?" yelled Bobby.

Jeremiah h_____d Bobby and raced over to him. "H_____. I'm h_____ at last.

Are you having fun?"

Bobby grinned and said "I'm having a gr_____ time. But th_____ is t_____ much

to do! I've b_____ly s_____n anything! I'm glad y_____ h_____."

"We can s_____ the rest of the f_____ together. Let's go!" exclaimed Jeremiah.

They grabbed th_____ candy and off they ran.

Use these words to complete the story:

week - weak	grate - great	pair - pear	chili - chilly	high - hi
there - their - they're	to - too - two	wait - weight	heard - herd	for - four
hear - here	bear - bare	fair - fare	see - sea	hey - hay
seen - scene	sent - cent	sew - so	eight - ate	you're - your
threw - through	fur - fir	wood - would	piece - peace	

The War in the Wood

Once upon a time, th_____ were t_____ b_____s who lived with th_____ aunt

deep in the woods. They owned a cottage beside a river. The woods were very quiet

and p_____ful, even in the winter when the trees were b_____ and the wind

b_____. The bears were very happy living there.

Not far from th_____ home was a gold mine, wh_____ the bears owned. The

b_____s w_____d work hard all day digging the gold o_____e from the ground.

Th_____ aunt worked too. In the mine office she w_____d w_____ the

gold on scales and ship it out.

Late one afternoon, a strange lady entered the office and peered about. "Which

w_____ to the gold mine?" she asked.

"Our mine is north of h_____, along that road," replied A_____ handing

her a map. "It takes half an h_____ to get th_____. Why do you ask?"

"_____ just want to see a real gold mine," cackled the old lady slyly. She

r_____ the directions on the p_____ of paper and stuck it into the

pocket of the dark bl_____ cape she w_____.

A_____ decided to follow the strange woman to the gold mine. "I just don't

trust that woman. She had no hair and really long fingernails! I wonder why she

really came h_____."

When she arrived at the mine Aunt could h_____ shouting and fighting. The

old woman was standing in front of the mine with her arms stretched out pointing at

the entrance. Each time she blinked her evil e_____ lightening bolts blasted

thr_____ the door. The frightened bears were yelling and banging things

around inside.

"Get out of h_____," they screamed.

As the w_____ raged on, Aunt exclaimed "Good grief! She is a w_____! I've got to stop her!"

A tiny R_____ Army A_____ scurrying thr_____ the dust gave her an idea. She grabbed a handful of dust, ran toward the mine, and thr_____ the dust into the w_____'s eyes, startling her. The dust made her blink and when she put her hands to her face, the lightening bolts zapped her!

"Come out h_____, boys. There's is n_____ danger now. The w_____ is over. She is gone, so we can have p_____ again."

Use these words to complete the story:

there - their - they're
two - too - to
bear - bare
peace - piece
blue - blew
which - witch
would - wood
ore - or
weigh - way
here - hear
I - eye
read -red
wore - war
aunt - ant
through - threw
no - know

Atlit's Lucky Day

The s_____ was just rising in the bl_____ sky. Atlit shivered as the wind bl_____ across the tundra. He pulled his hood over his thick black ha_____ and started to harness his ei_____ Husky dogs. His fingers were cold where the seal skin had worn out. He needed n_____ mittens. He a_____ the piece of blubber he had brought and prayed he wo_____ find good hunting. Last time he had been so embarrassed. He had only caught a few fish and his s_____ Ootah had brought home a walrus!

The team set out quickly. Atlit didn't want to stay out over night. It wo_____ be hard to keep warm because there w_____ be no w_____ for a fire. Trees do not grow on the frozen tundra. A long w_____ from camp, Atlit spotted a small h____d of caribou.

"Yippee!" he shouted.

Caribou are large animals and w_____ tons. One w_____ give lots of m_____ to eat, as well as skin for n_____ mittens. Atlit crept up and reached f_____ an arrow. He had to be careful because he had only brought four arrows. He was about to shoot when he h_____ a noise at his feet. An Arctic h_____ scurried past. Thinking fast, Atlit tried to grab it by its short stubby t_____. He missed the h_____ and tripped on some large rocks and fell, knocking the rocks over the cliff.

"Phew!" he said. Atlit was okay, but the noise had scared the caribou. They were gone before Atlit could fit another arrow into his bow.

Disappointed, Atlit went down to the beach to at least get some fish.

"I k_____ Ootah is really going to laugh this time!" he thought.

What a surprise he found! The rocks he had knocked over the cliff had landed on a large seal laying on the ice! He was lucky after all!

"Now," he thought, "as long as I don't meet a polar bear like Ootah, I will be all r_____. What a t_____ I have to tell everyone. Will they believe me?"

Use these words to complete the story:

sun - son	blue - blew	hare -hair	warn - worn
eight - ate	wood - would	new - knew	right - write
way - weigh	meet - meat	for - four	
herd - heard	tale - tail	know - no	
right - write			

allowed	aloud	
	Link-up: *loud*	
ant	aunt	
bare	bear	
bean	been	
	Link-up: *ea* as in *eat*	
blue	blew	
board	bored	
border	boarder	
break	brake	
chilly	chili	Chile
course	coarse	
died	dyed	
eight	ate	
	Link-up: *eigh* as in other measurement words (*weigh, height, weight*)	
fair	fare	
fir	fur	
for	four	
	Link-up: *our* = number words	
fourth	forth	
	Link-up: *our* = number words	
grate	great	
hanger	hangar	
hare	hair	
hay	hey	
heard	herd	
	Link-up: *hear* with *ear*	
here	hear	
	Link-up: *hear* with *ear*	
hour	our	
I	eye	
know	no	
	Link-up: *k* as with *knew* and *knowledge*	
main	mane	
meet	meat	
	Link-up: *ea* as in *eat*	
new	knew	
	Link-up: *k* as with *knew* and *knowledge*	
or	ore	

pail	pale	
pair	pare	pear
	Link-up: *ea* as in *eat*	
passed	past	
	Link-up: root word *pass*	
piece	peace	
pour	pore	
rain	reign	
red	read	
sail	sale	
see	sea	
sent	scent	cent
slay	sleigh	
some	sum	
stationary	stationery	
steak	stake	
	Link-up: *ea* as in *eat*	
sun	son	
tale	tail	
there	their	they're
	Link-up: *ere* as in *here, where*	
through	threw	
two	too	to
vain	vein	
waist	waste	
ware	wear	where
	Link-up: *re* as in *here, there*	
wait	weight	
	Link-up: *eigh* as in other measurement words (*weigh, height, weight*)	
way	weigh	
	Link-up: *eigh* as in other measurement words (*weigh, height, weight*)	
weather	whether	
weed	we'd	
	Link-up: (contraction) of *we would*	
week	weak	
wore	war	
would	wood	
	Link-up: *ould* as in *should, could*	
write	right	

A <u>pie</u>ce of <u>pie</u>

I h<u>ear</u> with my <u>ear</u>

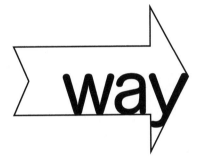

B<u>ears</u> have <u>ears</u>

witch

Make pictures of these hilarious homonyms.
Work with some friends and make up some of your own.
Share them with other groups.
Choose your favorites and make posters of them to post in the classroom.

a hairy hare	a bare bear	I ate eight _____	chilly chili
a furry fir	a pale pail	a pair of pears	some sums
a bored skateboarder			

Black Line Master 27 Hilarious Homonyms. *The Spelling Book: Teaching Children How to Spell, Not What to Spell* by Gladys Rosencrans, ©1998. Newark, DE: International Reading Association. May be copied.

This list gives the origins of some common English words. Their history, at times, explains their spelling, but always makes them interesting.

Silhouette: *a profile or outline portrait filled in with black*, comes from Etienne de Silhouette, the Comptroller General of France in 1840. Many cartoons were directed at him and silhouette became a word for a figure reduced to simplest form. It is a derisive reference to his excessive economic practices.

Candidate: It's origin is linked to the word *candid—to be white*. In ancient Roman custom those seeking office had to be candid (dressed in white).

Panic: In early times shepherds were often frightened by strange noises. They attributed these noises to the god Pan, the god of shepherds and hunters. Hence a fear of the unknown is *panic*.

Fad: like many others *fad* is really an acronym. It originally meant *For A Day*.

News: Early newspapers claimed they reported important events from all the parts of the globe. They originally printed the letters NSEW around a globe symbol. Eventually the symbol was omitted and the letters were written in a straight line: *NEWS*.

Tip: is another acronym standing for *To Insure Promptness*. Waiters in a London coffee house put a box bearing this inscription in a conspicuous place. Patrons were to deposit pennies in recognition of good service.

School: comes from a Greek word meaning leisure. A contradiction you say? In ancient times business hours were devoted to the state. Leisure hours were devoted to oneself—studying or schooling.

Salary: comes from the Latin for salt (*sal*). It originally referred to money allotted to soldiers in the army to buy salt, which was not plentiful, nor cheap.

Sandwich: was named after the Earl of Sandwich. He was such a devoted gambler that he had slices of bread with meat between them brought to him at the gaming table so he did not have to interrupt his playing.

Camouflage: came to our language from the French. It was adopted during World War 1 and means literally to *blow smoke into another's eyes*.

Spinster: In olden days, women did not marry until they had spun a full set of bed furnishings. Thus, during the time they spent at the spinning wheel, they were called *spinsters*.

Leopard: Greek and Latin zoologists considered the leopard to be a cross between the lion (*leo*) and the panther (*pard*).

Greenhorn: likens an inexperienced person to a young animal whose horns have just begun to sprout.

Coconut: the coco is from a Spanish baby-word which means *ugly face*. The black spots give it a somewhat ferocious face.

Cold Shoulder: English hospitality meant serving hot, juicy mutton. But when a guests stay was overlong, the butler was instructed to serve the mutton shoulder cold (*cold shoulder*) until further notice.

Corduroy: or 'corde du roi' (the king's cord) was given to soldiers for distinguished service. The king of France ordered his clothmaker to make a cloth to resemble the King's cord for him to wear.

Black Line Master 28 From Whence They Came. *The Spelling Book: Teaching Children How to Spell, Not What to Spell* by Gladys Rosencrans, ©1998. Newark, DE: International Reading Association. May be copied.

1. Cut out these words.

   How are they alike?

   Which words go together? Why?

2. Sort and paste them into groups on the sheet provided.

3. Give each group a name.

autobody	century	telepathy	telephone	aquarium
metric	telegram	audience	audible	televise
television	aqueduct	geography	geology	aquaplane
astrologer	automobile	autobiography	geology	astronomer
auditory	aquamarine	octagon	October	duplex
centipede	physical	manipulate	astronomical	duplicator
duet	telephoto	automaton	centimeter	audio
malaria	psychiatrist	barometer	phychopathic	psychology
psychic	thermometer	automatic	astronaut	malformed
octopus	manual	biography	duplicate	meter
manufacture	malice	malign	telescope	manuscript

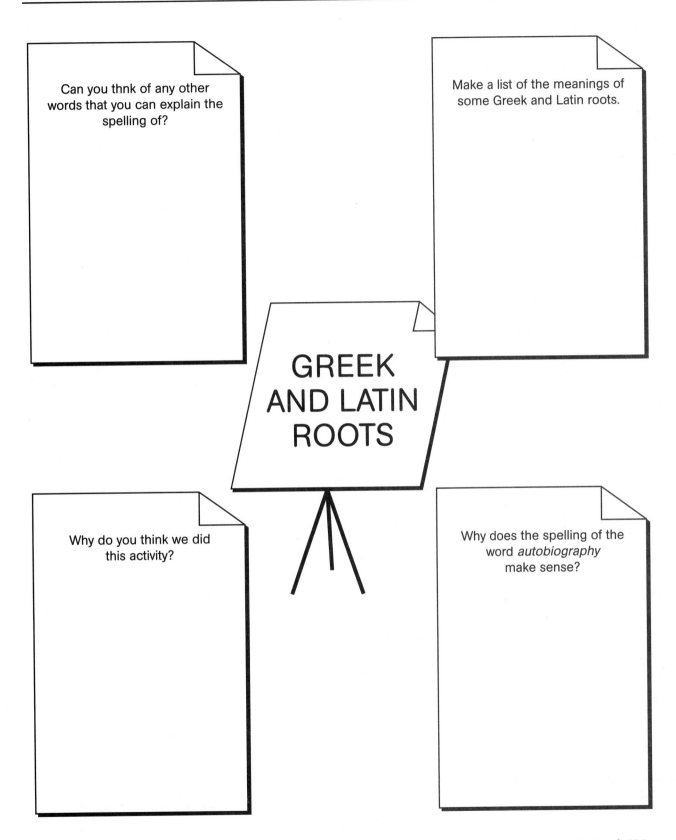

Can you thnk of any other words that you can explain the spelling of?

Make a list of the meanings of some Greek and Latin roots.

GREEK AND LATIN ROOTS

Why do you think we did this activity?

Why does the spelling of the word *autobiography* make sense?

Name _____

Date _____

Words:

Meaning

Words:

Meaning

Black Line Master 31 Making Meaning. *The Spelling Book: Teaching Children How to Spell, Not What to Spell* by Gladys Rosencrans, ©1998. Newark, DE: International Reading Association. May be copied.

Name _____

Date _____

Students: Read the following article about tarantulas and fill in the missing letters. Be prepared to discuss the missing letters after you have read.

Terrible Tarantulas

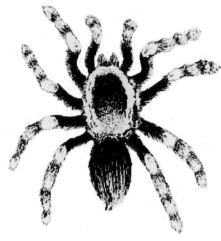

Tarantula__ are as old as the dinosaur____ and have not change____ much over the century___. There are approximate___ 600 different variety___ with about 30 kind__ live____ in the Unite__ State__.

All tarantula__ are hair__ and most are big— some huge! The large_____ are the bird-eat____ of South America. Some may make their home___ in web___, but all American tarantula___ live in burrow___.

Baby___ dig burrow__ of their own as soon as they leave their mother__. When a tarantula is hungry, it crouch___ at the entrance of the burrow, waiting to pounce on any creature fool_____ enough to happen by. At the slight_____ hint of danger, it scoot__ back into its hole.

Tarantula__ are deaf and near___ blind. But a tarantula can stay tuned-in to its surrounding__ with its thousand__ of hair__. Each hair act__ as a feel___ to pick up vibration__ and then reports them to the spider. Hair__ have other use__ too. When a tarantula is threaten___ from the back, it quick__ rub__ its hind leg__ against the top of its abdomen and then brush___ off a cloud of tiny hair__ which get into the eye__ and nose of the enemy, cause_____ a terrible itch.

Some movie__ portray tarantula__ as poisonous kill_____, but the ones in the Unite__ State__ are usual____ harm_____. They are so peace_____ you could keep one as a pet—**if you want___!**

Adding Endings

Group Members

_____

_____

_____

Words we rejected	Reason for rejection

We noticed that

BLM 36 Spelling Program Assessment Checklist

	usually	at times	seldom
Are my students enjoying their exploration of language?			
Are my students confident to share or talk about their spelling strategies?			
Is my assessment ongoing and based on authentic writing?			
Are my lessons planned according to what I've noticed my students doing, saying, or writing?			
Are my students engaged in short, daily spelling exploration?			
Are my students confident that errors or miscues are a natural part of learning?			
Are my students actively engaged in the learning activities?			
Are the activities connected with meaningful text and classroom learning?			
Are the activities a good match with the developmental level of the students?			
Are my students learning the strategies that good spellers use to spell new words?			
Do my students have opportunities to develop appropriately, including semantic, structural, and graphophonic knowledge?			
Are my students engaged in many and varied opportunities to write?			
Do my students write frequently in many different genre?			
Do my students have many opportunities to read and use language orally before writing it?			
Do my students see the spelling process modeled?			
Do my students have many opportunities to proofread their own work?			

Notes: